The Stapeley Book of
WATER GARDENS

The Stapeley Book of
WATER GARDENS

STANLEY RUSSELL

Illustrated by George Telford

DAVID & CHARLES
Newton Abbot   London

British Library Cataloguing in Publication Data
Russell, Stanley
 The Stapeley book of water gardens.
 1. Water gardens
 I. Title
 635.9'674   SB423

 ISBN 0-7153-8649-2

First published 1985
Second impression 1987
Third impression 1989

Phototypeset by ABM Typographics Limited, Hull
and printed in Great Britain
by Butler & Tanner Limited, Frome
for David & Charles Publishers plc
Brunel House   Newton Abbot   Devon

Contents

Introduction

After air and sunlight, water is mankind's most precious commodity. It is certainly the most versatile. But because we take its presence so much for granted we seldom pause to reflect that it covers the greater part of the globe, has provided a means of transport since the beginning of time, and plays a vital part in producing power and food.

In this volume we are concerned only with water at the domestic level, with the pleasures it can bring and how we can train it to provide us with a rich variety of entertainment in a garden pool or stream, as a fountain, a waterfall, and even indoors. For we do not even need a garden to taste such pleasures. An area less than $\cdot 6m^2$ (6sq ft) on a balcony, patio or in a corner of a room would still be enough to provide an endless source of interest. For wherever there is water, it becomes the focal point. It holds a magnetic fascination for all of us – from tiniest tot to elderly retired, we are enchanted by the movement of water.

Unlike soil, water does not, of itself, need fertilising. Nor is it ever too dry, too wet, or too hard for us to work. A pool, once installed, will remain for years, all the time demanding far less attention than any equivalent area of land. It does not need digging, hoeing or mowing, and maintenance is minimal.

Although water prefers to find its own level, in doing so it will submit to whatever way we want to play with it: cascading down a miniature waterfall, coursing gently through a channel shaped to our own design, or leaping and dancing in lively fountain displays. With the aid of lights it will turn any colour we wish. It brings a new dimension to any garden, and its mobility can be matched and enhanced by the gyrations of fish of all sizes, shapes and colours skimming or gliding below the surface in ever-changing directions, never really still yet relaxing to all who watch them. Another major bonus is the way in which water attracts wildlife. No other single feature makes such a contribution to the encouragement of birds, amphibians and insects.

There is a simple but enormously satisfying art in giving pond fish proper surroundings just as, for our greatest pleasure, the pool itself should be merged into its environment. For all their movement and colour, fish cannot appear at their best if they have to perform in a bare tank, with no plants to offer shelter from the sun or among which to play gentle hide-and-seek with us. More prosaically, there must be some form of plant growth to ensure a good supply of oxygen to keep fish alive and healthy. There are so many kinds of fish from which to choose – the common goldfish, shubunkins, Golden Orfe or the colourful Koi carp some of which are 1m (3ft) long, to name some of the most popular.

Even without fish, there is a further way of enjoying water in the garden – by marrying it with other ornamental features in the garden design. In the pool itself a wholly different world of plants such as the serenely beautiful water-lily will thrive and, nearer the water's edge, other smaller plants that like to get their feet wet and to be submerged except for their leaves and flowers. Around the pond land plants can flourish, the whole merging together as a scene of eye-catching effect and colour. Even the actual setting of your water

Photo 2 In this well-established country garden the pool surround has been chosen to complement existing stonework

display offers scope for imagination. Since a garden pool will almost certainly be artificial, it will have to be integrated into its immediate surroundings in some way. So you can set the scene as you want it – edging it with paving, cobbles, grass, or with plants all round.

And what of the night? Perhaps it is then, even more than by day, that the water garden really comes to life. Fountains leap in a beam of coloured light; underwater lamps illuminate the surface, bathing the surrounding plants in colours that give them fresh identity or cloaking fish in a new mystery as they go on their apparently aimless way. What a temptation to sit beside it all with a cool drink in the hand, or make a contribution to the evening scents with the appetising smell of barbecue cooking! Nor is one's enjoyment confined to sunny days and warm summer evenings. A water garden will provide interest all the year round. When the weather is mild, fish will greet you almost as warmly in January as in July.

Modern techniques have greatly simplified the task of installing a pool. The conventional concrete for bottom and sides has been almost entirely replaced by materials that are lighter, easier and quicker to handle, and which are far less prone to spring those irritating and mysterious seepages that so annoyed the pioneer pool owners. Preformed structures made up of glass fibre and laminated polyester resins, or some other form of plastic, are obtainable in shapes to meet most requirements, and all that is necessary is to dig out a hole that matches these contours.

Even simpler and generally cheaper, too, yet with a life expectancy of up to half a century, are the various grades of pool liner that come in sheet form, and which are made of synthetic rubber or plastic. The best are based on butyl, a tough material apparently unaffected by climatic conditions. These sheet liners enable their owner to give full rein to his individual tastes. They can be made to virtually any size and, given freedom from sharp stones or acute angles, will conform to whatever shape has been made ready to receive them. The actual task of installing them is amazingly simple. The weight of the water settles them in place and keeps them there.

Normally, a pool will be ready for use within a few days of being installed. It is then a case of endowing it with the trappings and trimmings that it merits as a key point in the garden. Just one word of warning. The new pool owner may well feel that an area of water, with a few plants and perhaps some fish, will satisfy all his ambitions. It will not. There is hardly any limit to the additions and embellishments available to provide untold extra pleasure.

This book is based partly on the author's own adventures but mainly on the experiences of professional experts who have spent years landscaping water gardens and installing all kinds of unusual features, but always with the aim of blending with the surroundings, whether mighty or minuscule, and always with the overriding consideration that the finished work must give pleasure for years to come. It aims specifically at putting these lessons into practice and at showing, in simple terms, how to set about choosing, siting, equipping and maintaining various kinds of water features, and at forestalling rather than solving the problems that are likely to arise.

The result should be a specialised water garden, tailor-made to your own needs and individual tastes, that will fascinate all who see it.

1 Choosing the Type of Pool

GENERAL CONSIDERATIONS

Very few of us have a natural pool or stream in our garden. Most of us would probably like one, or something nearly equivalent, and it is a fair bet that those who profess unconcern would be won over very easily if once they sampled the joys and fascinations of watching water perform its magic in the garden.

One consolation for the vast army of 'have nots' is that nowadays it is easy to install an artificial pond, even a stream, and place it in the best position to enjoy it. By contrast the natural variety will almost certainly be in the worst possible position – concealed in a shady dip, probably polluted by overhanging trees, and even liable to dry up during a spell of hot weather when it would have been of greatest use as a relief from the heat and breathless atmosphere of the rest of the garden.

Let us assume, then, that you wish to have an artificial water feature in your garden; whether you call it a pool, a pond, or a water garden is immaterial. What matters is that it will broaden your horizons immeasurably, and that you do not need a large garden as your passport to the delights it can offer. Indeed, you do not even need a garden at all. Forget all the general gardening conventions. The last thing you need is soil, except as a medium for aquatic plants. Your water garden can be on the terrace of a town house, on a patio or even in a free-standing container. Flat dwellers, especially in high-rise blocks, can be one up on their neighbours by installing a small water garden on the balcony; a flat roof is another good site. First, however, check the load-bearing capacity of balcony or roof. If you lack all these conditions you can, in admittedly specialised circumstances, have a water garden indoors – even a miniature one on a windowsill!

Water can be controlled exactly as you wish. Anxious as it is to go its own way, and find its own level, and shape up to the contours of its surroundings, it will however willingly conform to your reasonable desires. In short, your water garden can take any one of many forms. Your first essential therefore is to decide on the type you want. This may seem elementary, but it is not quite so simple as it sounds, and it is extremely important. For on your decision may rest the fate of your entire garden for the foreseeable future.

Is the pool to be formal or informal? Do you want it sunken or raised? Do you wish it to be ornamental or purely functional? Is it to be with or without plants, a fountain, a water-course, or lights? The choice is bewildering, and the first steps must be taken cautiously. Whereas a conventional part of the garden can be made to change its appearance year by year if desired – flower-beds becoming vegetable plots and vice versa, and even the lawn taking on new shapes and dimensions – your water garden, once in place, and especially if it is the sunken variety, will probably remain there for ten, twenty or even fifty years. You will most likely add to its attractions by installing lights, a fountain or other moving water and, of course, fish and plants if you have started without any of these really worthwhile ingredients. But moving it, changing its shape or enlarging it means a lot of hard work. It will therefore pay you to think years ahead.

Photo 3 Formal raised pool with fountain and symmetrical planting scheme

Budget to get the basic pool you really want and, if no more funds are available, embellish it as you go along. Final achievement tastes all the sweeter for waiting: far better that than limiting your horizons at the start and feeling frustrated ever after. But whether you are waiting or doing it all at once, make financial and structural provision for all the auxiliary installations when you are building the pool. If you are having a surface pump you will need special pipework and housing for the 'waterworks'. You will need to lay cables for a pump and for lights (in a conduit) and, if you are having a waterfall or stream, you must provide a pipe to run the water from the pool to the outlet. It sounds a lot, but these are time-consuming operations as afterthoughts once the original pool is complete; incorporating them in the original work takes only a few extra moments. Foresight in your planning is the key.

RAISED OR SUNKEN?

Although the debate will centre on whether your water garden is to be formal or informal, perhaps the first question to be settled is whether it is to be raised or sunken. Obviously, a sunken pool, where the water is at or a little below ground level, is the more natural looking, and therefore more informal; there are, however, forms of raised structure that are definitely worth considering. Although not so natural looking as the sunken types, they do have some advantages and can look very attractive.

In the short term, raised pools are easier to construct than sunken ones, for less soil needs to be excavated and found a new home. In the long term the raised or half-raised pool – its shell generally constructed with bricks and/or stone – is also a boon to the disabled and elderly, as any maintenance work requires far less stooping. Given an appropriate design, the surround can provide a neat sitting-out area. Above all, there are compelling practical considerations. In the event of a storm, there is no prospect of the soil being washed down into the water, or flooding in the subsoil causing major disturbance. Even more important, the surrounding wall will present an impenetrable barrier against any weedkiller or fertiliser being leached into it from the surrounding area, with the risk of damage to plants and fish.

On the other hand, the hard work involved in digging out several cubic metres or feet of soil for the more natural-looking sunken pool can be repaid, if done properly, by an improved landscaping effect that will give the site additional beauty and interest. The spoil (the amount of soil excavated) can be used in a surrounding rock garden or for a waterfall – a feature that might look incongruous in a raised structure. Generally, a sunken pool will be slightly cheaper than the raised version, for you will be spared the cost of the necessary walling, though this will be countered to some extent should you wish to surround your sunken water garden with paving or embellish it with a rock garden.

Again, the long-term aspect is important, though it may not be so obvious at first sight. Plants and fish will be more comfortable in a sunken pool than a raised one, for the water temperature is more constant. Day and night through the seasons a certain amount of warmth will be provided by the soil, which will buffer any sharp changes of temperature.

Above all, the sunken pool gives far more scope for design, since it is easier to form into any desired shape. Though both types can accommodate a fountain, a sunken pool is really the only kind that offers the inestimable benefits of contrasting heights and consequently greater eye appeal that comes from the provision of a waterfall, a rockery, a bank on which plants can grow, or even an adjacent bog garden for special plants that thrive where it is damp underfoot.

FORMAL OR INFORMAL?

At this point you have to make your next decision – whether you want your water garden to

Photo 4 Informal sunken pool set in corner of garden with rock garden

be formal or informal in character. There are advantages and disadvantages with both kinds. First, what is the meaning of formal and informal? My own quick rule-of-thumb definition is that formal must be symmetrical and will appear manmade with crisp outlines, whereas informal means as nature would have made it.

Steer clear of the temptations of compromise. It is both technically and aesthetically wrong to try to mix formal and informal aspects, although there have been exceptions. I know of cases where specialist designers, going against all their professional knowledge and judgement, have humoured a client wanting to do just this and have been agreeably surprised at the result. The only logical surmise is that in some way the surrounding terrain lent itself to both styles, and consequently the formal and informal elements, instead of fighting, merged with the background and with each other.

Such conditions must be rare. Normally, the sensible plan is to decide which type you want, and stick to the rules governing that

13

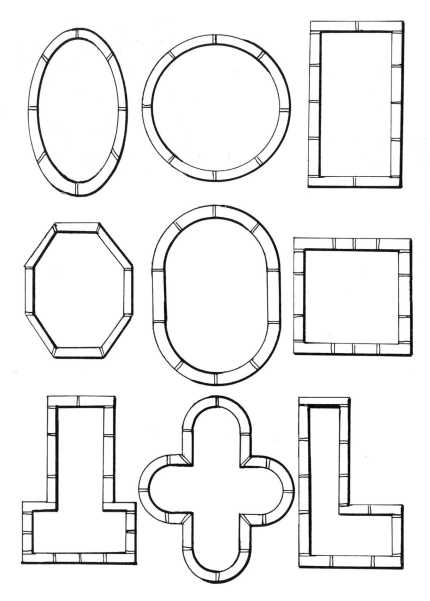

Fig 1 Formal pool designs for the water garden

style. Meandering informal waterfalls or streams, for instance, should only be associated with informal pools. A waterfall linked to a formal pool should have straight channels and uniformly stepped falls. Fountains are perfect in formal pools, showing off their manmade genius; but are not so much at home in informal surroundings.

Personal choice must be the final arbiter; and if you are happy with the result, little else matters. But it must be stressed again that yours is the ultimate responsibility for how the water feature is going to look for years to come, so do give most careful consideration to all these preliminaries, for once committed the effect is permanent. Minor changes can, and should, be undertaken once your water garden is well established, but a mistake made now, whether in shape, type, design, size or layout,

14

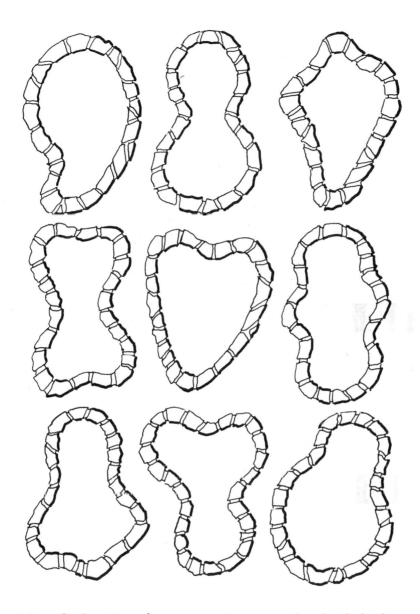

Fig 2 Informal pool shapes for the water garden

will be with you for years, and it will be no good putting a brave face on it if you sense that family and friends are secretly shaking their heads over your folly. There is only one piece of advice I would dare to give as to formal and informal pools but it is important – study your surroundings, and design and site your water garden in accordance with what you have. So let us examine the choice in greater detail.

As with a formal flower bed, a formal pool has to conform to tradition. Its shape and its edges must be clearly defined, following a set pattern, whether square, oblong, circular or elliptical (Fig 1). Its function is to preserve an air of tranquillity, of reflection. Indeed, many formal pools are placed so that they can catch the greatest possible reflection from the sky, providing nature's own version of a picture in water colours. It must be perfectly balanced:

an unconventional touch or placing, such as a fountain positioned off-centre, destroys the symmetry.

Formal pools imply a tidy mind, in design and maintenance. They are, on the whole, neater and probably easier to keep spruce than the informal type. Most are paved to the edge, thus saving the inconvenience of mowing right up to the water and unsightly grass clippings floating on the surface for a time. A formal pool will look marvellous if you approach it over a long wide area; in other words, it will be the jewel in the formal setting. A fountain would be an ideal embellishment – nay, a compulsory one. Formal pools also suit patios; one set against a south wall will add much interest.

Certainly, there can also be a case for an informal feature amid a large area, but it would be better at the side or near a corner, where you could still have a fountain and, even better perhaps, a waterfall, which would not be so compatible with a formal layout.

A formal pool, then, is one for showing off; an informal one is more likely to provide quiet intimate enjoyment for the viewer.

It is more likely to convey an impression of a devil-may-care approach, aiming at cheerful spontaneous enjoyment. But there is nothing informal or devil-may-care about the way it should be planned. On the contrary, it is probably much harder to make the informal pool look informal. Like a good actor rehearsing his lines and movements over and over again until they sound and appear natural, you must be prepared for some alteration in the planning stage. Your efforts and patience here will be well repaid.

An informal sunken pool will scorn straight lines and right angles. Its shape will be comparatively irregular, perhaps with a few rocks to add an extra dimension and provide a home for small plants and, for best effect, spaces between these plants where close-cut grass goes to the water's edge. Designing such a feature is not just the work of five minutes (Fig 2).

Both types have very strong appeal, and many garden owners will have a tremendous mental struggle before deciding which to adopt.

Page 17 Water garden with established plants and ornamental fountain feature

2 Landscaping the Pool

POSITION OF POOL

Your water garden is destined to be a work of art, fashioned by you and nature in collaboration to bring life, movement, reflections and colour, day and night through the seasons. But if it is to be the picture of your dreams it requires a worthy frame.

Perhaps even more important than its style – formal or informal, sunken or raised (or half raised) – is its position and size. It must be in proportion to the garden as a whole, or at least as much of it as is in view at the same time. It is impossible to lay down any hard and fast rule as to just what percentage of the garden your pool should cover, for local conditions will determine just how much space is available. One can only point out obviously ridiculous aspects such as a tiny pool, say 1·8m x 1·2m (6ft x 4ft), at the far end of a half-acre lawn or, at the other extreme, a pool that fills the entire garden leaving room only to walk, very carefully, round the edges.

The garden as a whole should be designed with curved paths beckoning you on intriguingly to find new vistas at each turn. Ideally, this sense of discovery would also apply to the water garden, lifting the veil a little at a time, but space limitations in most modern properties thwart such ambitions. I suggest, therefore, that unless you have a very large garden you go to the other extreme and site the pool as near the house as you reasonably can, so that at all times you can look out of the downstairs windows and see what is going on. You may have plants, fish, underwater lights, a fountain or a waterfall, and for maximum enjoyment you will want to have them all in view if possible (the underwater lamps, of course, should not be seen other than from close to the water's edge: it is the effect that matters). The advantage of having the pool near a path is mentioned on page 28.

At all times the water garden will be the most observed, the most admired, and probably the most envied, part of your garden. It will be leading a double life. Outwardly, it will convey an atmosphere of restfulness and tranquillity but in fact, if you have stocked it with fish – as assuredly you will do eventually – it will be teeming with life and movement, which will become apparent as soon as viewed from close range. That is one of the charms of a water-garden feature. You never see a rosebud burst into bloom, or a passion flower open to reveal its breathtaking markings, but nobody will have to wait for hours beside your pool or water garden for something to happen once you have it fully installed, planted and stocked with fish. So do place it where you miss as little as possible of the activity.

There may well be a clash between what you want for your own enjoyment and what is best for the pool itself, its contents, and its management, so compromise may be necessary. Ignore anything you may have been told about being sure to have your pool close to a tap. Once filled, it will need very little topping up; and this can easily be done with a hosepipe.

Page 18 (above) Half-raised water garden built into sloping ground; *(below)* informal water garden fed by a waterfall

There are at least half a dozen criteria for picking your spot.

1 Avoid overhanging trees.
2 Keep out of the shade of houses or walls.
3 Site it, as already mentioned, where it can be seen from indoors.
4 Consider the position of electrical installations.
5 Avoid waterlogged areas.
6 Plan for shelter from prevailing winds.

As keeping away from trees and shadows is important, it follows that you will seek a sunny spot. Site the pool to ensure the sun shines on it most, if not all, day, not just for part of it. Apart from the pleasure of sitting in the warmth beside your pool (with a sun umbrella if necessary for temporary shade) this has practical advantages. Water-lilies need sun: they should have ten to twelve hours a day at the height of summer. Fish, too, benefit; although they are susceptible to rapid changes in temperature they can shelter in the shade of the lily leaves.

Avoiding overhanging trees is given such priority because here lies a trap for the unwary, in that potential damage from them can easily be overlooked. Indeed, the thought of sunshine glinting through the leaves, creating a pleasing dappled effect on the water, is extremely tempting, and for the greater part of the year they may give no trouble. But think of autumn, and falling leaves dropping into your pool. Few things are more lethal to its contents than decaying leaves, whose decomposition creates gases that are definitely harmful to fish and no good for plants. In conventional gardens, some gardeners use them as a mulch to protect plants remaining in the ground through the winter. Where there is

a pool they must at all costs be cleared from the surface. Spread a covering net over the water to collect them, or sweep the top with a fish net. Leaves of any kind are a menace in the water. On a lawn, worms will eventually pull down and recycle any that are not swept up, but this does not happen in a pool. There they become a wet rotting mass, in no way beneficial to the water life.

It may be argued that where there are fish and especially plants already in the water or around its edge, decomposing waste matter is already present. This is true; but the point is that generally the pool and its inhabitants are self-balancing. The pool can deal with its own decaying matter quite adequately, and the chemical balance of the water changes imperceptibly with the gradually changing natural content and conditions. If a sudden influx of 'foreign' leaves blows into it the balance is disturbed. This leads to an excess of methane gas, a main reason why fish sometimes die in winter. In particular, keep well away from Laburnums and Laurels. Both are notoriously poisonous. Seeds and leaves alike are lethal, and should any fall into your pool they will prove toxic to the fish and probably some of the plants as well.

Less obvious is what may happen below the pool – unseen, longer term in its development perhaps, but equally menacing. Trees grow, and over the years the roots spread and thicken, with devastating effects. The risk may seem small, but it does exist. The danger here is that you may not notice it until too late, though a clue is damage to a nearby party wall or fence. You may escape if your pool has a flexible liner that adjusts to the gradually changing contours, but don't count on it. There is a definite risk of disaster if your pool has a concrete base or sides, or is a prefabricated resin and glass-fibre affair; cracks could be caused that would quickly drain the water away, and there is little consolation in knowing that this material can sometimes be repaired.

Photo 5 A charming effect is achieved by this well-landscaped pool planted with a good variety of marginal and bog plants

Visibility (or viewability) from the house, is largely self-explanatory and has already been covered. As the pool is such an important feature of the garden you will doubtless ensure that it can be seen from all points.

The pool's relationship to electrical installations is important. If you are planning for a waterfall or fountain you will need a pump. If you want lights to give you after-dark illumination, you will need electricity, which will also work the pump, so a power source should be fairly close. It is useful to install a power point (preferably a double socket) in a handy position inside the house, or in a conservatory, garage or shed, to avoid having to go out of doors late at night or in inclement weather. A double socket will provide facilities for using an electric mower, cultivator or hedge trimmer without affecting the working of pump or lights. Low-voltage equipment is available, which will provide adequate lighting and power for most purposes and is virtually accident proof. But wherever electricity is being used, indoors or out, I strongly recommend fitting a power-breaker unit, which trips and cuts off the current immediately anything goes wrong.

The fifth point concerns the risk of having water in the wrong place. Constructing a pool in a low-lying area – a little dell or valley, where the water table is very near the surface, possibly even making use of a natural brook – sounds ideal for a 'natural' informal pool. Marginal and moisture-loving plants should thrive there, but so will natural vegetation, which will take a lot of controlling. In fact, shun this spot like the plague. The brook can overflow, the water table can rise suddenly or heavy rain fail to drain away. You are left with a flooded area, which is definitely not the kind of pool anyone wants. If the site is liable to flooding the water will not only bring in unwanted surface debris, but will also undermine the pool's foundations.

In case there are any lingering regrets about ignoring the apparent advantages of natural sources, bearing in mind that millions of fish and plants thrive in or near rivers and streams, it must be stressed that natural running water does more harm than good in the water garden. It upsets the balance of the pool, keeps the temperature down, and lilies and many other plants will never grow as they should.

Finally comes the question of shelter. Many plants are susceptible to cold draughts; water-lilies in particular are affected by the disturbance caused by wind (as well as drops from a fountain) ruffling the water surface. Try to ensure that the bitter north and east winds are not given a direct run at the site.

Always with a wary eye on leaf fall-out, consider a hedge or shrubs or some form of screening. A windbreak is effective for a distance roughly four times its own height, which will give you a good idea of how to allocate your space. As much shelter as possible should be given, but the north and east aspects are the most important. Marginal plants, especially the strong-growing varieties, can also be used on the windward side to give protection.

A sloping site should not be dismissed out of hand, indeed a water garden sunk into a bank or slope can be an extremely attractive feature, but there are dangers. As I have already pointed out, surplus water running off the lawn or elsewhere can bring with it weed-killer or other chemicals harmful to fish and plants. Care should be taken when constructing to ensure the slopes are reshaped to avoid this.

There is also the practical aspect of making sure that the pool is absolutely level. Very careful and frequent consultation with the spirit level will be required to ensure the correct build-up or excavation all round its edge; it will look unsightly if the water level appears higher at one side or one end than the other. On a sloping site a raised or half-raised pool is probably an easier proposition, though whether it is aesthetically satisfying is another matter.

SIZE AND SHAPE

With type and position settled, the next big question concerns size and shape. If you are having a moulded pool, the shape will be pre-determined for you. With a flexible liner you are free to use your creative skills. However, you should avoid complex shapes as they cause excessive creasing and wastage of material. Designs should generally be smooth and without kinks and narrow channels, which will largely be lost when the pool is established. So keep the design simple; the work will be easier and the final effect more pleasing. This applies whether your pool is to follow formal architectural convention or reflect the informality of a freehand sketch. The controlling factor as regards size will be the overall amount of land you have at your disposal, or at least the amount of it visible at the same time as your water feature. Proportion is what matters. If, when finished, the pool blends with the rest of the garden and presents a nice balance, you can feel satisfied and can look forward to infinite pleasure.

Designing the best shape and size of pool can seem quite a daunting problem at first. In conventional gardening, we often begin digging without being absolutely certain we have chosen the best place for what we want to grow. That may not matter too much; but if one made such a mistake when digging out the pool area, the results would be permanent. Luckily, there are ways of meeting the problem half way without going to a lot of, possibly wasted, physical effort.

First, get your ideas down on paper. Make a ground-plan sketch of the outlines of your garden – the fences and boundaries, the position of the house (including the windows from which you will see the pool), the garage, greenhouse and any other outbuildings, plus permanent features such as trees and other immovable objects. Draw all these to scale; squared graph paper will be helpful in this exercise (Figs 3 & 4). When you have filled in these features you will be able to see, surprisingly clearly even in a small-scale rough sketch, how much space you have available for your pool. You will also realise that there are many ways of combining your dreams with the practical limitations with which you have to cope.

Some of us are not very good at drawing plans, but there is a simple alternative way of seeing how a scheme will fit in; in fact, I recommend it as a back-up in any case. Select your proposed site and mark out the pool outline with a length of rope, hose, or cord (a long clothes line will do), making sure it can be seen from a distance. Then go back to the house and study it, preferably from an upstairs window. View it from every available angle, judging both size and shape. You will get a very good idea how it will look in perspective, when the work is finished. Don't be in a hurry to rush out and begin digging. Watch your outline for some hours, on a sunny day if possible, to see where shadows are thrown as the sun 'moves round', and adjust your rope accordingly. This is the simplest way of ensuring that you get the necessary maximum amount of sunshine. A drawing can be only to a very small scale; your outline marked out life-size on site will steer you away from the vital errors of sharp turns and angles and narrow channels.

But even this exercise will tell you only part of the story. For your actual water area is only part of the whole, and you should allow roughly half as much space again, perhaps more, for the surrounding amenity, whether you plan a formal pool with paving all round or an informal one with plants, a rockery (perhaps with a watercourse) or a bog garden. At this stage you have several options; you are not irretrievably committed if you alter the outline 15cm (6in) or so here or there. Provided you are not overdoing it, it is far better to make the area larger than you feel you need rather than keep it down to a set size. The larger it is, the more interesting it will be; moreover, the greater the area of water the more constant the temperature will be. It will

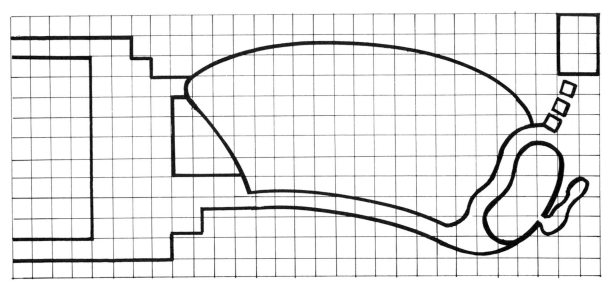

Fig 3a Planning an informal water garden

also be easier to keep clear balanced conditions. Neither fish nor plants like sudden and frequent changes, which will happen in a small pool. True, a larger area will mean more digging, but that will provide more spoil to create a more interesting rockery and waterfall.

There is a danger that enthusiasm for the project will run away with you, so a word of warning. It will become the focal point of your garden, so leave plenty of room for you and your visitors to get round it in comfort. Roses and other shrubs may form a picturesque background, but make certain they are not so close as to block the view. If your thoughts stretch to a summer-evening poolside barbecue, with its out-of-this-world cooking odours and flavours, plus the enjoyment of lights, fountain and fish, you will need plenty of room in which to appreciate all these wonders.

Nevertheless, having taken all these factors into account, I suggest devoting as large an area as possible to your water garden itself. Even if your current budget does not run to all you want for it, don't lower your sights, or let present difficulties swamp or kill your ambitions. Take heart from the fact that water, the most important ingredient in your plans, is also the cheapest!

One early decision will be whether to include a rock garden and/or watercourse (a waterfall gushing out from the top of a bank or a stream appearing perhaps half way down). This will entail raising the soil level to form a bank during the construction work and is the natural home for spoil dug out during excavation for the pool. Before you dig the first spadeful, think of how you see the finished job, so that you can keep all the spoil as near as possible. Keep turves handy for any new grassy slopes, and make a separate pile of topsoil. Use the subsoil at the bottom of the rockery and shape this to suit your layout, then spread the topsoil over the whole rockery – you cannot expect plants to flourish in poor subsoil.

What experts call the balance of a pool is important; for a clear algae-free pool, harmony must be established between the plants, fish and surface area of water. Size is a major factor in this equation. The minimum size recommended to achieve the necessary balance is a surface area of $3 \cdot 7m^2$ (40sq ft), representing a pool $2 \cdot 4m \times 1 \cdot 5m$ (8ft x 5ft). This area should

Fig 3b Garden as shown in plan opposite

result in clear water conditions, given the right supporting factors. A small pool contains very little water. There is minimal movement, so it becomes extremely vulnerable to changes in the nature or quality of the water. In this respect, a small concrete pool is particularly dangerous, for even a limited amount of cement can raise the pH value of the water to a level intolerably high for fish. Rapid temperature fluctuations, as we have seen, also cause them great discomfort.

A garden pool does not need to be very deep; the benefit of the fish is the main consideration. The minimum recommended is

38cm (15in), but this should be considered only for small pools of less than 2·3m² (25sq ft) area. Normally 45–60cm (18–24in) is enough: 45cm (18in) is sufficient for up to 9·3m² (100sq ft) surface area and 60cm (24in) up to double this amount. Above 18·5m² (200sq ft) you should have at least one part that is 76cm (30in) deep. These are general guidelines; for very cold areas you may wish to have a greater depth of water and also where the pool is made specifically for Koi carp (see Chapter 7).

Freezing, and how it affects fish, is the main worry. Ice locks in all the waste gases that normally escape through the surface, and this can cause fatalities. Fish can survive in surprisingly low temperatures, provided gases can escape and they are not stuck in a solid block of ice. Clearly, a very shallow pool will freeze over very easily. But over the greater part of Britain it is rare for water to freeze more than about 15cm (6in) deep.

This consideration of depth purely for the benefit of fish is covered more fully in later chapters. Aquatic plants can look after themselves quite easily in 45cm (18in) of water, and that includes even the most vigorous water-lilies which are very accommodating. If you set them in water 90cm (36in) deep they will still settle down but they will be just as happy in little more than half that.

Fig 4 Planning a formal water garden

3 Preparation for Digging; Lining Materials

There are several ways of holding water in a hole in the ground. In essence, all are a kind of waterproof lining. They will not stop evaporation, but are intended to prevent leaks or seepage. Generations ago pools and ponds were made of puddled clay. Then came concrete. The twentieth century has provided us with reinforced glass-fibre or semi-rigid plastic 'basins' moulded to an appropriate shape and, above all, with sheet liners of various grades of polythene, plastic and synthetic rubber. The virtues and faults if any of each of these two basic methods of construction are described later so that you can make your own personal choice.

MARKING OUT AND TOOLS

The starting point, however, for whatever kind of sunken pool you require is the same: you have to dig a hole! So having marked out the site with hose or line, the next step is to make temporary markings for the time you will be at work, by pegging out the area. This is done very simply by driving in very short stakes of wood to a uniform height all round the perimeter. If you have bought a preformed pool liner, such as glass fibre, you will need to be accurate in your measurements and the amount of soil you remove, for the liner must fit snugly on its base. Any cavity below it will be a source of trouble, for once the pool is filled, the weight of water will force it out of shape unless properly supported, and the consequence of this need only be imagined.

It is also important to ensure that there are no stones or sharp edges that can cut into the liner, and this applies particularly to the sheet types. It is not important if you are planning a concrete pool, for which you will need some gravel or aggregate; but a liner pool, of whatever type, will need as soft and comfortable a bed as you can provide. So allow for a good layer of sand – 2·5cm (1in) minimum – on the base to act as a buffer or sponge, absorbing any stones that lift or other changes in the soil profile.

Tooling up for the job may sound elementary, but is important because a few moments lost while looking for a missing piece of equipment at a crucial time could spoil the operation. Obvious essentials are the normal gardening standbys of spade and fork for digging, rake for smoothing out and a wheelbarrow to carry the tools and remove the spoil; a mattock or even a pickaxe will be needed if the ground is hard, and some planks or good stout mesh to act as a 'road' and thereby make barrow work easier and less likely to cut up the route from site to soil tip. You will also need a board as a guide when digging straight lines if you are preparing a formal square or rectangular shaped pool. A spirit level is essential – a builder's level is suggested for speed and convenience because it is larger than the domestic type. You will also need a tape measure or a stick marked in metres or feet and yards, according to which system you are using.

If possible, site the pool close to an existing path, for convenience both in the making and in subsequent enjoyment. Although it is very pleasant to walk across a lawn before breakfast or on a dry warm summer evening, grass can become very damp through rain or dew. A path, whether of brick, concrete, stone or paving, leading from the house to the pool does provide a tempting method of moving from one to the other, so if you are starting your garden from scratch it will pay to plan your pool and the pathways at the same time. In this case it is best to complete the paths first.

But please do not lay out your paths like a motorway. A straight concrete path will look ghastly. Functional, certainly; but who wants purely functional aspects here? A winding concrete path, one made of bricks or crazy paving, or one where grass areas and paving stones alternate, are all acceptable. But never force the eye to wander straight from the house to the pool. A water garden epitomises subtlety and relaxation, never a get-there-at-all-costs attitude.

SHEET LINERS

Sheet liners are flat sheets of synthetic rubber, plastic or polythene which will fit into any pool design, of any size or shape, giving maximum flexibility to meet individual requirements. The current popularity of garden pools is undoubtedly due very largely to the development of this kind of material, which can probably be traced back to the late fifties and early sixties, when sheets of polythene were laid in holes in the ground and filled with water – a development of the much more cumbersome tarpaulin that had formerly been used for holding a small volume of water in case of emergency. Those early polythene sheets were tremendously successful, although they had to be (and still are) regarded as being only a cheap and short-lived expedient in bringing a water-garden feature into anyone's garden.

It was not long before a superior grade of sheeting took over as a pool liner. Nowadays we have quite long-lasting PVC; better still, there is butyl. This is a form of rubberised sheet developed during World War II as a means of transporting various kinds of liquid (it could even contain acids), and its potential use in the leisure field quickly became apparent.

Naturally, it is more expensive than ordinary polythene or PVC, but is far longer lasting. There are various grades, available under a number of trade names. One is guaranteed for a remarkable length of time, no less than twenty years; but in normal circumstances is expected to last far longer than that. It has a conservative estimated life of fifty years even when in daily use, at which it seems destined to outlive all other forms of sheet liner.

There is superb irony in the fact that this material is recommended for lining a (supposedly permanent) concrete pool that has started to leak. Empty the pool, dry it off and clean it, then lay the material over the concrete, cutting it and shaping it to fit. It is a very good way of doubling (probably more than doubling) the life of a pool very quickly, with negligible expense. And though there may be comparatively few cases where a plastic sheet comes to the rescue of several inches of concrete, the example shows the tremendous flexibility, in all senses, of these sheet liners. They are virtually limitless in their application. Many a reservoir holding millions of gallons is lined with this material – sufficient reassurance for the householder looking for a reliable liner for his garden pool!

A good liner will provide many years of trouble-free pleasure and service, so careful consideration should be given to the different types available. Of course you will have to pay more for the best, but when you consider the area involved (only a few square metres or yards) and the years it will remain in place, you may agree that here is an occasion for saying 'hang the expense'. This is, after all, the most important part of your pool equipment, and it is vital to make the correct choice according to your needs and ambitions.

Most sheet liners are produced to set widths and are cut to length as the customer requires. Butyl, for instance, can usually be supplied off the shelf up to an area of 30m x 6·7m (100ft x 22ft). A larger size than that still presents no problem: it can be made up in a matter of seventy-two hours. Befitting its flexibility, this material offers the purchaser a wide range of options. It can be prefabricated to various shapes including box shapes, circular with vertical walls, L-shapes, or even hexagons. Naturally, this works out a little more expensive than buying the normal flat sheet, but you have the luxury of having it specially and exclusively made to whichever of these shapes you want.

Besides being so adaptable, butyl has a remarkable resilience to weather conditions. It will withstand any temperature from −40°C (−40°F) to +120°C (248°F) – a range far greater than is likely to be found in any civilised conditions. It has the further advantage of being virtually unaffected by ultra-violet light, ozone, sunlight, and even oxidising agents. It is also resistant to bacteria and fungal growth, and because of its toughness it can withstand a great deal of friction from abrasive elements, flexing or tearing, and even some degree of puncture. Accidents can happen and, should the material ever be punctured, a repair kit consisting of patching tape and adhesive is available. The standard product comes in black, but there is a luxury version in which a stone-coloured sheet is laminated on a black one.

I have referred to butyl at some length because of its outstanding properties, but there are other sheets that warrant consideration. The already mentioned PVC sheets are usually cheaper, but there is one important difference in their qualities. Butyl is practically impervious to anything and everything and is remarkably flexible, especially considering that it is fairly thick. PVC, no matter how good the grade, will eventually break down against ultra-violet light. This may take several years, but you must be prepared for it to happen in due course.

A very good bet here is double-laminated PVC, which is barely half the price of butyl. It is a good sturdy material, blue or black on one side and stone-coloured on the other, has been treated to resist fungus and bacteria attack, and is unaffected by frost. Again it is very adaptable as regards shapes and sizes and is quoted in areas up to 7·3m x 4·9m (24ft x 16ft), or can be made larger given a few days' notice.

In between these two is reinforced PVC sheeting, which has a high-tenacity nylon mesh between two laminated PVC sheets. This, too, is dual coloured, so can be used with either blue or stone side uppermost. It comes in rolls 1·2m (4ft) wide and is made up to any required size by a high-frequency welding process. It is claimed to offer considerable support, strength, and tear resistance. In small sizes there is very little difference in price between it and the standard butyl. In fact, for use purely as a pool liner, it is not easy to justify the extra cost of the nylon-reinforced compared with the non-reinforced version. And it cannot match butyl, which itself costs little extra. Reinforced PVC is claimed, correctly, to be immensely strong and resistant to stress, but for our particular use the added strength of nylon is of little advantage, as the material will not be taking the strain of any weight. It will merely be lining a hole, resting on the ground, so no stress is involved; the soil provides the support. No long-term benefit is gained, either; in fact some reinforced-PVC-lined pools have broken down after a short time, while non-reinforced ones were still in good condition.

Clearly, the initial outlay of the lining is an important consideration when costing a pool and its accessories. But the material to hold the water must be bought and installed as the first priority; there cannot be any form of pool or water garden without it. So think ahead to the time when all is nicely established and the fish and plants are thriving. With cheaper liners there may come a day when the liner cracks, the water runs away, and you are literally left high and dry. In that event the whole water feature has to be ripped out and, apart from the expense and inconvenience of relaying, it will be months before the wound has healed. It is not an experience anyone would wish to undergo too often. It is at times like this that one realises how spending a few pounds extra at the outset would have proved a really worthwhile investment – one that would in effect have lasted a lifetime.

Having delivered this little homily, I must add that if you are having to work to a budget, the unreinforced laminated PVC can prove a very worthwhile compromise. It should certainly last for a decade, and probably a great deal longer. Laminated PVC sheets, of whatever type or grade, are usually two-coloured – beige (or stone) one side and blue or black on the other. As already mentioned, you can use it either side up, and there is a natural temptation to expose the lighter colour. This is a mistake, for it can cause too much reflection. Keep this side next to the soil and look happily on the dark side. It absorbs light and heat and will more quickly become lost to view once the pool is established.

At the bottom of the range of sheet liners is the original-style polythene, which brought so much pleasure to the pioneers of small garden pools a couple of decades ago, but which has now been left far behind. Although manufacturing techniques have improved since those early days, this material is still comparatively fragile. It is a cheap way of trying out an idea or experimenting, but its use should be considered only where a temporary pool is required, as when cleaning out a major pool and needing a home for the fish. Or you could use it for keeping fish fry and for breeding live food. If you do buy polythene sheeting, insist on at least 500 gauge (125 micron), and remember that it will still have to be laid double.

Polythene and PVC have the common fault that they crack under the effect of the sun. Normally, this happens either where exposed to the air or, even worse, just below the water-line. While PVC can sometimes be patched, there is no way polythene can be treated per-

manently, so the whole installation must be scrapped and the pool completely relined. Real-term value is reflected in the price. Polythene costs slightly less than half the cheaper laminated PVC. Equate this with the estimated length of life and service – two years as against ten years – and you get a fairly accurate version of where true value lies.

To some extent you can guard against premature failure by ensuring that the pool is properly made in the first place – that is, by being level all round. So often the level on one side is below that on the other, with consequent exposure and cracking. The secret is to keep the water right up to the top all round, to protect the liner as much as possible, as all exposed areas are extremely vulnerable. With butyl, however, exposure does not seem to matter; experience so far indicates that there are no ill effects from an area being left dry.

MOULDED LINERS

The preformed moulded type of liner comes in two main types: the more expensive and immensely strong (though light) reinforced glass-fibre moulds and the plastic semi-rigid ones at half the price or less.

Most newcomers to pools, when thinking of moulded liners, automatically consider the glass-fibre types. Made up of laminations of glass fibre and polyester resins, they are strong and durable with a life expectancy of ten and probably more years, they will resist frost and ice, and algae seldom appear round the sides. They are available in various shapes, styles and sizes, and most are contoured to provide steps or ledges on which to grow marginal plants. They offer the added convenience of ready-made edging, artificial though it may look – plain, simulated rock, or simulated crazy paving.

The built-in simulated rock or paving flange adds to the overall area and will have to be allowed for when digging. It is a good idea to take off the top 5cm (2in) of turf all round to accommodate this flange if your pool is to be

sited in a lawn, so that it will not protrude above grass level and prove a menace to the mower.

In one way these preformed types appear to be the answer to the lazy or unimaginative man's dream. Because they come in a predetermined shape, all he has to do is dig out a hole to fit the contours. He does not have to bother too much about the kind of design he would really like. This ready-made luxury of having the ideas and design already worked out has, however, to be paid for by meticulous preparation. With a sheet liner, any miscalculation made in the contour of the excavation, especially low down or at the bottom where it will be out of sight, matters little. As it fills with water the sheet will obediently follow and fit in snugly to whatever shape has been made for it. With a moulded pool, unless you excavate or back-fill exactly to its shape you will leave a gap where the weight of water – ·0283m³ (1cu ft) of water weighs 28·3kg (62½lb) – could cause distortion and subsequent weakness, cracking and loss of water. Lavish use of sand as padding is indicated!

Besides this they have other disadvantages when compared with flexible sheet liners. Because of their fairly complicated manufacturing process and their bulkiness in transport, they are much more expensive. Also, because they are preformed, they and not you are the masters of the situation; there is no scope for individual design except in the edging and finishing. Another awkward factor is their deceptive size – although they can appear huge when standing upright at a garden centre, they appear to shrink to about half this size when actually installed in a garden. As mentioned previously, size plays an important part in creating balanced water conditions, and it can be difficult to maintain this balance in most of the moulded pools available.

As with sheet liners, there is a budget version of the preformed pool. These are known as semi-rigid, and are vacuum-formed from tough weather-resistant plastic material. As their name implies, they are more flexible than the bonded-resin types, and may not be so strong. But no liner of any kind, whether sheet or preformed, should be expected to carry any part of the weight of water unsupported. The whole structure should lie comfortably on its bed so that the weight is borne by the ground.

In due course the materials from which these semi-rigid types are made will fall prey to ultra-violet, so don't expect too much from them. Nevertheless, because of their comparative cheapness they can represent a good bargain and should provide years of enjoyment. You will, of course, have the same problems in making the bed as with the rigid glass-fibre types; you must get the excavation and subsequent back-filling absolutely perfect if you are to avoid distortion, stress and fatal leaks.

There are two other ways of making a pool, both outmoded by the advent of moulded and sheet liners – concrete, and puddled clay. As they cannot be bought ready-made for the job I have left them out here, but they are described in the chapter on Sunken Pools, which follows.

Summarising our examination so far, which method do you prefer – fitting a sheet liner to your excavation, or making a hole to fit a prefabricated container? If you are buying a preformed pool, whether glass fibre or semi-rigid, you will be able to study the various shapes and designs available either from a catalogue or by visiting a supplier; but you will be restricted to the range on offer, with no chance of adapting to your own design.

Photo 6 Glass-fibre mould with paved edging

Photo 7 Small PVC cascade waterfall mould

33

Settle on your size and design before you order your liner, whether it be a sheet or moulded type. Buying a liner first and then digging the hole to suit is the wrong approach here, and almost certain to lead to disappointment. Once you are satisfied with its site, shape, size and how it will blend with the surroundings, you can get down to the actual construction. This is shown in detail on pages 41, 46 & 47.

Page 35 (above) Informal raised water garden with fountain feature and varied plants; *(below)* water garden with watercourse running through rockery and crazy paving edging

4 Sunken Pools

You have decided on all the preliminaries – where your water garden is to be sited; its shape, avoiding sharp turns in its outline; its size and type, whether formal or informal; the material from which it will be made; and have taken account of 'optional extras' such as fountain, waterfall, fish, rockery and lights. You have remembered you will have to make provision for laying cables and pipes. At this stage you must decide on the type of edging to be used because this may alter the profile of the pool and may also change the size of the lining required, as explained in Chapter 6.

To some extent you are lucky if you are making a new garden from scratch and suffering only the agony of having to hide the builder's rubble. The answer to this problem is simple; the rubble can be used as the base for a rockery or watercourse, and so help to provide an attractive extra elevation. But it is far more likely that you will have to agonise over sacrificing part of the lawn. Here, too, something can be salvaged to provide an amenity, for some of the turf can be used as edging round the pool or to patch worn parts of the lawn, or even to start a new one after levelling off and filling in a flower- or vegetable bed no longer required.

Strip off the turf as evenly as possible; pieces 60cm x 30cm and 5cm deep (2ft x 1ft x 2in) are a convenient size for handling. They are also ideal to use when planting aquatics (see page 114). You can spread the rest of the excavated soil over the garden, but remember that some of it will be subsoil and therefore unusable except as base material. If you have planned a rock garden and waterfall the excavated soil will naturally form the basis for this. Keeping the topsoil separate, use the subsoil as the base and contour this to shape. The topsoil can then be spread over the top.

Where pools are constructed on sloping ground the surrounding area can be contoured to ensure the site is level (see page 18). If this is not practicable, a low wall can be built to retain the higher-level soil. Another alternative is to build up walls at the lowest side to make a partially raised pool, which can prove an attractive feature (Fig 5).

FLEXIBLE SHEET LINERS

Flexible sheet liners are by far the most suitable type for most people – easily available in all sizes, cheaper than the pre-moulded liners, easier to transport, and far less demanding in the preliminary work. When you have decided

Page 36 (above) Caltha polypetala; (below) Eriophorum angustifolium (Cotton Grass)

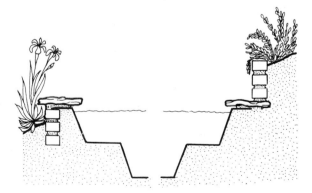

Fig 5 On sloping ground the levels can be adjusted with retaining walls

Fig 6 The size of the liner is not altered by the inclusion of a marginal shelf

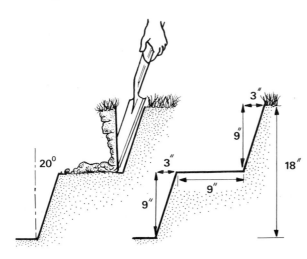

Fig 7 The sides of the excavation should be sloped inwards as shown

on the size and shape of your proposed pool, measure the overall greatest length and greatest width. The third measurement needed is the depth of water, referred to in Chapter 2.

To discover the size of sheet you will need, double the depth and add this to both length and width. Thus a pool with maximum length and width of 2·7m x 1·8m and ·5m deep (9ft x 6ft x 18in) will need a sheet 3·6m x 2·7m (12ft x 9ft). For overall measurements of 3·6m x 2·7m and ·6m deep (12ft x 9ft x 2ft) you will need a sheet 4·8m x 3·9m (16ft x 13ft). In other words, if you double the surface area, you less than double the size (and cost) of sheeting, which is another good excuse for making your pool as large as you can. You won't need to allow extra material for an overlap because the inward-sloping sides make the pool dimen-

sions less at the bottom than the top. This will automatically give surplus material to make an overlap at the top edge.

Do not fear complications in your calculations should you wish to build a ledge 23cm (9in) wide to take marginal plants (see page 39). The amount of liner required for a marginal shelf (shown as a dotted line) exactly matches the amount of liner required if a marginal shelf is not included (Fig 6). These calculations are for a pool with paved edging. Pools with other types of edging may require more material, please refer to Chapter 6. Raised pools with vertical walls will also need extra material, see Chapter 5.

With all the dimensions of your pool now fixed, you can begin excavating. Your hose, rope or cord marking the perimeter should be pegged firmly in place, for this will be your template and it is a good idea to cut just inside that outline. This has the advantage that when you see the actual hole you can make slight adjustments without penalty. As the old joke says, you can always add to a hole by taking away from it; but you cannot reverse the process in this case. Dig at a slight angle. This part of the operation is rather tricky, for you have to go down at an angle of about 20 degrees. At 23cm (9in) down your overall area measurements will be 8cm (3in) less than at the surface (Fig 7). Where the soil crumbles or is very sandy the angle should be increased, see Chapter 7.

There are three reasons for making this slope. One is that it reduces the risk of the sides caving in. The second is to ensure that if the pool freezes in winter the ice can expand without causing damage. The third is that at this angle the sheet liner, which will follow your excavations so obediently when weighted by water, will settle very nicely into its basin and give an overlap at the sides, to be held in place by paving slabs or other forms of edging.

As you dig round the edge make constant reference to the spirit level across both length and width of the hole. The edge must be kept level at all costs; if the ground slopes you will have to excavate more deeply on the higher side or end, to compensate. If either length or width is too great to accommodate your spirit level, even when resting on a straight-edged plank, drive sturdy pegs around the edge of the pool, making sure they are all at absolutely the correct level, and use these as 'staging posts'.

It is advisable to plan for a few marginal plants (we are, after all, thinking in terms of a water garden). These need to have their feet in the water and their heads in the air, so you must construct a ledge for them – 23cm (9in) is the universal depth and width, so at 23cm (9in) down you merely cut a ledge 23cm (9in) wide and resume your inward-sloping progress to the bottom. This marginal ledge is made where required, or can continue all round the pool. In any case you will find it easier to construct the shelf all round and afterwards cut it away as required. If you plan an edging of rock stones, these will have to be bedded onto this ledge; so you will need to allow at least another 15cm (6in) in width when cutting the ledge (Fig 8).

For most pools it will not be necessary to dig down more than ·6m (2ft), unless specifically for Koi carp. Normally this depth is enough for a surface area of up to 18·6m² (200sq ft) – larger than any of the rooms in many modern houses! Naturally, you will remove any flints or other sharp objects as you dig (it is surprising how often you find pieces of broken glass and china or pottery), and any stones should also be deposited elsewhere.

Lay an inch or two of sand along the bottom to act as a cushion in case settlement under the weight of water does bring the liner into uncomfortably close contact with an unsuspected object lying just below – a 2·7m x 1·8m (9ft x 6ft) pool will need about 100kg (2cwt) of sand. A coating of damp sand round the sides will also be helpful in smoothing out any rough areas. As an additional precaution, a sheet of polythene or specially made polyester

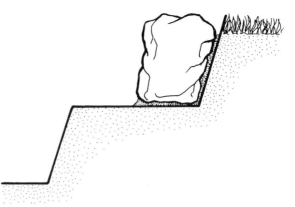

Fig 8 Where rock is used as edging, the marginal shelf must be made wider to accommodate the stone

matting will help to ensure security from punctures. Do not use wet newspaper for this operation, as sometimes advocated. It does not offer any protection against sharp stones or flints; and if laid over a stone it will only decay, leaving the stone in contact with the liner.

Before laying the liner in position, make sure you have a means of anchoring it temporarily. If you have planned for a paved edge, a few paving stones placed at strategic points will prove helpful; otherwise some bricks or tiles will be adequate. You will almost certainly need help in this version of laying an outsize tablecloth.

Lay the liner over the pool so that the overlap along each side is as equal as possible, and the same at each end – equal all round, in other words. Don't pull it taut: just let it sag gently into the excavation. Then connect the hose and run in the water. You will be in for a busy hour or so easing some of the weights and making neat pleats where the liner creases. Be careful to keep the overlap even all round so that you do not lose an edge or a corner (Fig 9). You will find some wrinkling as the liner fits snugly under the pressure of water into the excavation, but this is not serious and probably will not be noticed once the pool is well established and the edging completed.

Fig 9 Rectangular, or informal pools, with sharp angles should be filled to the marginal shelf, and then surplus material gathered at the corner and pleated to make a neat fold

When the pool is full the top edge should be level all round. Don't be disheartened if it is a little out; at this stage it can be packed if necessary to make it level. There should be some excess material left all round the edge. Trim this off with scissors, leaving about 10cm (4in) all round the outline of the pool. These offcuts will be useful for placing under rocks or stepping-stones if you wish to add them later.

Your pool is now ready to receive its 'beauty treatment' – the edging that provides the first step in its emergence as one of the most attractive aspects of your garden. That part of the process is dealt with in Chapter 6.

POLYTHENE LINERS

The basic principle here is very similar to that of laying flexible sheet liners. The pool area has to be dug out in precisely the same way, but because the material is not of such high quality as the butyl and PVC liners you have to take extra precautions against damage and breakdown. Also, as there is little stretch in this material, it should be laid and loosely fitted into the excavation before water is added.

Generally, polythene is not so thick and lacks the resilience of the better liners. An old trick here is to fold the material over and use it as double thickness. Clearly, you will use much more material this way and it will not last so long as the better sheets, so the apparent saving on cost could easily turn out to be false economy.

GLASS-FIBRE LINERS

These are strong and well made, and have all the attributes of a tailor-made piece of equipment. You do not need to make any calculations as to how much extra you must allow for the overlap, for it comes already provided. All you have to do is to ensure that you have sufficient 'rebate' in the surround to accommodate it comfortably.

You buy them either with a plain edge or with a flange made to look like rocks or paving stones. They have already been described in some detail in Chapter 3, so if you are con-

Photo 8 Installing a moulded pool: the excavation is checked for stones and a 5cm (2in) layer of sand is spread, levelled and compacted on the base

Photo 9 The pool is placed in the excavation and checked to ensure the top is level across the width and length

templating buying one you will already know the advantages and disadvantages.

Again the basic principle is the same: the hole has to be dug to the size you need. But before starting work order some fine sand from your builders' merchant – for most pools ·25 tonnes (¼ ton) will be sufficient. Dig the hole approximately the same shape as the pool but about 15cm (6in) larger and 5cm (2in) deeper than the pool and lay a 5cm (2in) bed of sand on the bottom as a cushion (see Photo 8). Settle the empty shell on this comfortably, and with a spirit level check that the edge is level (see Photo 9). Then back-fill all round the sides with finely tilled soil and sand, so that your glass-fibre mould is adequately cocooned.

When back-filling, add water to the pool at the same rate (see Photo 10). Do this in stages: add 10cm (4in) of water and back-fill to a height of 10cm (4in) all round; then add another 10cm (4in) of water and back-fill a further 10cm (4in), and so continue to the top. This method ensures stability. You cannot back-fill without water, for the back-fill can push in the pool side, creating distortion. Conversely, you cannot fill with water without

Photo 10 The pool is gradually filled, at the same time back-filling to ensure the shell is well supported, particularly under the shelves; the surrounds are then levelled in readiness for laying the edging

back-filling as you go.

This business of making a comfortable bed for a preformed liner (and, for that matter, for a concrete construction which would be susceptible to any ground movement) is far more important than most people realise. We all know something of the power of water, physically as well as aesthetically, but most of us seldom allow for its weight. Using the garden watering-can gives us no idea at all. Carrying a full 22·7 litre (5 gallon) container whilst camping, or trudging back and forth with emergency supplies after a pipe has burst, is the only way most of us are likely to come to realise its sheer dead-weight.

There will be a considerable weight on the bottom of the pool when it is filled. A container of whatever nature 2·4m x 1·5m (8ft x 5ft) – the smallest practical area for a pool – and ·6m (2ft) deep takes 2,273 litres (500 gallons) of water weighing over 2 tonnes (2 tons), so it is easy to imagine what might happen were any part of the bottom unsupported.

This risk does not, of course, apply with the far more flexible sheet liners, as I have explained. The soil takes the weight, with no air pockets to provide hidden stress points. But the moulded types lack the flexibility, so accuracy is essential. Mistakes can be expensive. Even when you feel satisfied, watch carefully for any settlement as you fill the pool, and add soil or sand wherever necessary to provide solid support for the shell. This is the reason behind the technique of gradually adding water and back-fill at the same time.

This brings me to what I regard as the major plus-point for these prefabricated shells – they can look very good as raised or semi-raised pools (see Chapter 5) and the preparation is nothing like as tiresome as with sunken pools.

SEMI-RIGID LINERS
Compared with glass-fibre units these are fairly flimsy and therefore need slightly gentler handling. However, the method of constructing a pool with them is precisely the same: the hole must be dug and back-filled just as meticulously.

CLAY AND CONCRETE
Compared with the modern materials and methods we have been discussing, these two ways of making a pool are really impracticable for the average garden; but they are time-honoured methods so have at least an academic interest. Although laborious and time-consuming, they can give you the satisfaction of having done all the work yourself without assistance from modern manufactured parts.

Puddled-clay Pool
Making a puddled-clay pool (pond is perhaps a better description in the circumstances) is a reversion to a very old craft, still practised in certain parts of Britain as a cheap on-the-spot means of containing water. It is in fact the basis of our canal systems.

Normally, heavy clay subsoil is anathema to the gardener – horrible sticky gluey stuff, heavy as suet pudding in winter and hard as concrete in summer. But if you have some in your garden, you can turn 'potter' and make some kind of duckpond from it by beating it hard and forcing and ramming it into the shape you want. You will also require several other things: a good clay subsoil, and a thick well-firmed lining of good fine clay. It follows that you cannot choose your site for this operation, for the cost of buying-in sufficient loads of clay would really be prohibitive.

Assuming that you have a natural site and the necessary depth of clay, you can (after a lot of effort) get it reasonably smooth, and it will hold water – for a time. But come a dry spell, the water evaporates, the clay thus exposed to the air shrivels and cracks, and any plants and fish are left stranded. If you are prepared to top it up, daily if necessary, you can certainly have a natural-looking pool that costs nothing for construction materials. But don't torture yourself by counting the cost of time and effort spent on construction and maintenance!

Concrete Pool

Concrete is the other traditional means of keeping water within a given area. It has served mankind well, and is relegated to a minor position here only because it has been outmoded by products that are lighter, quicker, easier to handle and more reliable.

If you insist on having a concrete pool, you will have to dig it out not just to the appropriate area but a further 15cm (6in) or so extra all round, representing the thickness of the concrete, plus an extra 15cm (6in) in the base for the hardcore foundation and, if you are doing the job properly, a reinforcing agent. That can mean a lot more work. You will also have to mix cement, sand, gravel (aggregate) and water, judging the amounts of each ingredient exactly unless you can find some use for a mass of hardened surplus concrete when you have finished.

The usual mix is 1 part cement to 2 parts sharp sand and 3 or 4 parts aggregate (crushed gravel). There is a slight complication in working out exactly how much of each ingredient you will need, for although your calculations have to be done in cubic measure, cement is sold by weight. Reckon on a 50kg (1cwt) bag as being ·03m³ (1¼cu ft) and you will be about right. A concrete pool 3m x 2·4m and ·6m deep (10ft x 8ft x 2ft), which is really a very modest size, will require about 500kg (10cwt) of cement, ·7m³ (25cu ft) of sand and say 1·1m³ (40cu ft) of aggregate (you can always find a use for surplus gravel!). For every 50kg (1cwt) of cement you will also need a 1kg (2·2lb) bag of waterproofing powder.

All the materials must be thoroughly mixed before you add the water, and at this point all mathematical and rule-of-thumb calculations will desert you, because there is no set ration of water. Climatic conditions could have some effect and you must go on guesswork or

experience. The only advice I can give is not to make the mixture too wet and thin: this can cause air bubbles, weaken the concrete, and lead to leaks. Incidentally, the addition of water reduces the volume of your mixture by about 25 per cent.

You can save yourself a lot of trouble by ordering a load of ready-mixed concrete from a specialist supplier. Given the appropriate details, they will work out how much you need and deliver it to your door in its wet state, ready for use. If you decide on this method, get help with carting and laying. The concrete will dry out fairly quickly, especially in hot weather, and there will be little chance of finishing the job single-handed. Avoid working in either frosty or heat-wave conditions; in the latter case the labourers will quickly become exhausted and you will need to keep the unused concrete malleable by covering with a wet sack or giving an occasional very light spray.

The base goes down first, reinforced half way by steel or wire mesh. This may sound an exaggerated precaution but, as already pointed out, water is very heavy and there could well be soil subsidence that is no fault of yours, so you will need a thick sturdy buffer to minimise the effects. Before the concrete hardens, scratch it all over to provide a key into which the walls can be set and also for the final top coat or rendering.

Years ago wooden shuttering was used to hold the walls in place while setting. While this may still be necessary on some larger structures, you should be able to avoid this chore by sloping the sides and using a stiff mix that will set quickly. This gives an added bonus in that if ice forms during the winter it will normally expand without causing damage to the structure. The slope will be much more gradual than for sheet liners – 45 degrees is the steepest that can be considered and you may have to settle for less.

Bearing in mind the weight of the soil you have excavated and the mixing and heaving and laying of the concrete, you may feel entitled to a rest once it begins to set; but you have not finished yet. Scratch the sides while still malleable, for your cementing has left only a rough surface, and you still have to apply the rendering, or finishing coat. This involves a mix of 1 part cement to 3 parts of sand plus, this time, 2kg (4·4lb) of waterproofing powder per 50kg (1cwt) of cement, all mixed to a stiffish paste with a little water and laid as smoothly as possible on the sides and bottom. You are not plastering a room, so the result will not be satin-smooth and water will cover most of it, but make a presentable job.

The testing time comes after the cement has set. Fill the pool and leave it for a few days. If the level does not drop all is well: it is waterproof! If not, you must empty the pool, let it dry out and coat it thoroughly with a special paint to seal it – this will also seal in the lime at the same time. If the pool has passed the waterproof test, the normal curing process to neutralise the lime will last several weeks and involve several fillings and emptyings. You can short-circuit this by brushing over with a proprietary product which seals in lime. You will be able to stock the pool as soon as this treatment is complete, and will undoubtedly feel you have earned your reward when at last you can relax and watch the fish and plants.

A consolation after all this effort is that concrete is immensely strong. In theory, your pool should last a lifetime, but its strength could also be its undoing. For it has little tolerance; unlike some other substances, concrete cannot give gracefully under pressure. Perhaps the greatest tragedy in this respect is that concrete is so unpredictable. Even the best engineers in the world have difficulty in waterproofing it completely. Though the risks of serious failure may be remote, it can crack through frost or subsidence, and nobody is really to blame for the failure. It may only be a hairline crack, but the water will seep away and have to be topped up with irritating regularity.

Though I must admit to a certain (and undoubtedly masochistic) enjoyment in working with concrete and a sense of achievement when finished, I have to say that with all the modern and easier methods now available a concrete pool is not a good idea for most gardeners. There may be rare circumstances where such pools are acceptable, or even preferable, but these constructions are beyond the scope of the average householder.

Nevertheless, there are situations where concrete can make a valuable contribution to the surroundings of a water garden. Well-laid paving or setts, for example, are a great improvement on the traditional plain concrete path. A number of admirable leaflets and pamphlets are published showing ways of using concrete in the garden. Their content is beyond the scope of this book, but may provide ideas for a number of permanent and trouble-free features.

Page 45 A beautifully landscaped stream gives a feeling of tranquillity to this large garden

Page 46 Pool construction using a liner (*left to right, top to bottom*):

a Lay a rope or hose to the required shape and size, adjusting until all aspects are satisfactory

b Start digging, but always cut inside the outline to allow for final trimming and shaping; leave marginal shelves where required 23cm (9in) deep

c Insert short wooden pegs 90–120cm (3–4ft) apart round pool and use a spirit level to ensure that the tops are level; it is important to make sure that the top edge of the pool is absolutely level as the water will immediately show up any faults

d After final trimming and shaping has been completed, check the depth and width of the marginal shelves and inspect the sides and base of the excavation for sharp stones or roots

e Place a cushion of sand 1.25cm (½in) deep in the bottom of the hole, and work extra sand into any holes or crevices which may have been made by digging out stones

Page 47 Pool construction using a liner (*left to right, top to bottom*):

a Drape the pool liner loosely into the excavation with an even overlap all round and with stones or blocks placed as required on the corners and sides; commence filling with water

b As the pool fills, ease off the stones at intervals to allow the liner to fit snugly into the excavation; some creasing is inevitable, but many creases can be removed by stretching the lining as the pool fills

c When the pool is full, trim off the surplus lining leaving a 10–12·5cm (4–5in) flap temporarily secured by pushing long nails through the lining into the ground

d Rectangular pools can be edged with pre-cast paving; informal pools can be edged with broken slabs but natural stone paving is better and should be laid on a bed of mortar 3 parts sand to 1 part cement

e Ideally the finished pool should be emptied before planting and stocking with fish; this is imperative if cement has been dropped into the water

5 Raised and Half-raised Pools

So far discussion has centred almost entirely on the 'orthodox' type of pool, where the surface of the water is no higher than the level at your feet. Submerged pools undoubtedly form the vast majority, whether they be huge reservoirs for public water supply, swimming pools, or embellishments for the garden. Since all natural pools also fall into this submerged category, I suppose we should accept that these are the kind most suited to the environment. But man can occasionally improve on nature and, although raised or semi-raised pools may not be as nature intended, in some instances they offer greater benefits. A far from minor consideration is that a raised pool is so much more helpful to elderly people, and particularly to the handicapped of any age.

There are other reasons, practical or aesthetic, why a raised pool can be a more tempting proposition than a submerged one. Building up some kind of structure to form a watertight basin instead of digging a hole could prove to be easier, especially on a sloping site, and would have the additional advantage of preventing garden chemicals or debris being washed down into the pool. Other possibilities come to mind, beyond the mere banking up of soil to form a container for a liner. Stone- or brick-faced raised pools are always an attraction, the clean lines of a formal pool being

particularly impressive. Such a construction would look ideal on a patio, and if backing on to a dividing wall you could arrange for water to appear from a jet fixed into the latter. The apparently casual shape of an informal pool can also acquire extra distinction, particularly if the stone has a rugged appearance.

The construction method I am about to describe is virtually the same for a raised or a half-raised pool. A fully raised pool can have its base on level ground (or a patio), with walls built up to the equivalent of about seven courses of brickwork in height. A semi-raised pool need be only three or four courses high, but unless you want only a very shallow depth of water (not recommended) you will need to dig out an appropriate area to the required depth as with an orthodox sunken pool.

USING A FLEXIBLE LINER
You could build a single wall of brick or stone, hiding the liner overlap under the capping; but by far the best way, although it involves a doubling of effort, is to make a 'cavity wall' type of surround. There are two ways of doing this; but either way your walls should be given a foundation, though this need not be more than about 10cm (4in) of concrete on to which the bottom courses are laid.

One method is to build the outer wall of ornamental stone and the inner one of bricks or stone or cement blocks. Make sure they are absolutely level with each other, so you will need to use a spirit level (Fig 10). Estimate length, height, and width of each skin: your builders' merchant will be able to work out the quantities of material you require and also

Page 48 A delightful watercourse with waterfalls which formed part of the joint Stapeley Water Gardens/Blooms exhibit at the Liverpool International Garden Festival in 1984

Photo 11 Informal raised pool with bell fountain, groups of marginal plants and water-lilies

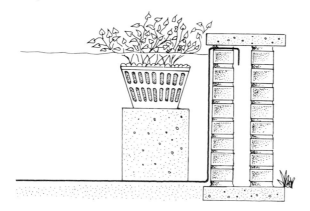

Fig 10 A raised pool with the liner fitted inside the inner wall; marginal plants are supported on blocks placed in the water

recommend the appropriate grade and quantity of mortar. Remember that you must allow for cutting some materials to produce the requisite bonding at the corners.

You will need coping stones for capping the walls. Not only will they keep out damp, dirt and debris; they will also hide pipes for water and cables for lights and fountains. Ideally,

your coping should overlap by about 1·5cm (½in) on the external wall and about treble this amount over the pool edge. For this reason you should select your coping before you build the wall; the width of the capping will determine how far apart the walls are to be built.

A formal pool is more likely to be rectangular in shape, so you will have to master the techniques of building return walls. You can, of course, have a square, oblong or L-shaped pool (Fig 11), or even a circular one.

Laying the liner is comparatively simple; as with submerged pools it is laid over the area and filled gradually, any necessary adjustments being made as you go. The surplus liner material is led over the top of the inner wall and into the cavity; the weight of the coping will hold it in place. Rectangular and square pools are easily fitted with a flat sheet and only require a fold at the corners. Round and complex-shaped pools may give rise to excessive creasing and wrinkling, and for these it may be advisable to have a flexible liner prefabricated, which will virtually eliminate this problem.

The second method is to build the inner wall on top of the liner, which is held as if between two skins (Fig 12). This has the advan-

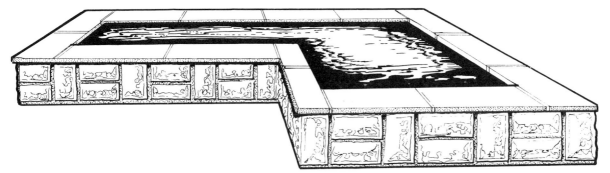

Fig 11 An L-shaped formal raised pool

Fig 12 A raised pool with the liner fitted between the walls; marginal plants are supported on blocks

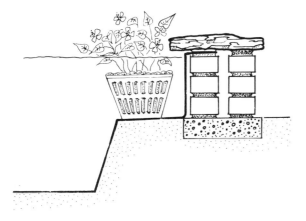

Fig 13 A half-raised pool with the liner fitted inside the inner wall; (see also Fig 51)

tage that if evaporation causes the water level to fall the liner is not exposed, only the attractive brickwork can be seen. Such a pool erected in a public place is also less prone to vandalism, particularly if the base is covered with a layer of concrete. As both inner and outer walls will be visible they should be of the same materials; and although good-quality bricks can look attractive, ornamental stone will produce a better effect. Because the inner skin is laid on the liner, clearly you will not be able to build directly onto a foundation. This need not cause alarm the coping will tie it to the outer wall.

First you need to construct the outer wall; then lay the liner onto the base of the pool, making certain the sides are equal all round. It will be annoying, after laying two courses of blocks, to find that you have 1m (3ft) of liner at one side but only ·3m (1ft) at the other. Stretch the liner slightly to remove creases and wrinkles: then build the inner wall directly on the liner. Work from outside the pool rather than inside to eliminate any chance of puncturing by standing on sharp pieces of stone or brick. If you must work on the liner make certain that it is adequately protected.

Housing marginal plants is easy if you use either of these methods. You simply stand blocks 23cm (9in) high and wide in the pool to form the ledge on which the containers will stand. Remember, however, that because the walls are vertical and not sloping you will need

51

Fig 14 Raised or half-raised flexible liner pools can be surrounded with a retaining rockery

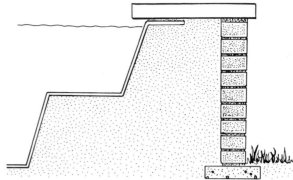

Fig 15 A raised pool using a rigid moulded liner, surrounded by an ornamental wall; this could be supported by a retaining rockery instead of the wall (see Fig 64)

to allow an extra 23cm (9in) of liner on length and width so that it overlaps the edges of the pool.

Half-raised pools are constructed in exactly the same manner but the shelf is on ground level and this eliminates the need to use blocks to form the ledge for marginal plants (Fig 13). Again, remember to allow extra for the liner, this time 15cm (6in) on length and width.

Informal pools can be constructed in exactly the same way as formal ones except, of course, that the shape is different, reflecting individual taste. Although obviously it is harder to build a wall than to dig the outline of a hole to the same informal shape, one consolation is that apparently a large number of amateurs find they have less trouble building a curved wall than a straight one! This method certainly has advantages on sloping ground, where the stonework can be used to build up the lower level of the pool.

There is much to commend raised pools to the home gardener, especially if he is a keen do-it-yourself enthusiast who wants a neat professional finish to his work. But perhaps their greatest appeal is to owners of buildings that are used by the public. Suitably decorated with plants, they can make a very attractive improvement to an entrance hall or foyer. They are virtually self-contained. The coping,

apart from its main task of hiding the ingredients and providing a façade, can also be used as a sitting-out area, and if height and area is planned in advance might even take small picnic tables for meals and barbecues. No artificial means will be required to cover either the overlapping of a sheet liner or the flange of a moulded one as this is built in as part of the construction.

An informal pool can be given a more natural look by surrounding it with a rockery effect. The inner skin is built and the liner put in place by either of the ways described, but the outer wall is in the form of a retaining rockery, planted with heathers or alpines. This method also can be used for either raised or half-raised pools (Fig 14).

USING A MOULDED LINER

If anything, it is easier to construct a raised pool using a moulded liner although, as previously mentioned, they are limiting in size, shape and design. As with flexible liners, these pools can be raised or half-raised and surrounded by a wall or retaining rockery.

For a pool surrounded by a retaining rockery, the glass-fibre or plastic shell should be placed on the ground; in the case of the half-raised version it should be let in to the required depth. In either case the shell must

Photo 12 A sink garden with aquatic plants

be laid on a firm level bed of sand and be completely supported, and the top edge must be level all round. Some 12–15cm (5–6in) of water should be run in to settle the shell; soil can then be built up around the pool making certain the planting ledges are well supported. More water can be added gradually, at the same time compacting the soil that has been built up around the pool. To retain the soil, rock stones are dug in around the perimeter and the pockets of soil planted with rock plants and heathers. Keep a careful watch for settlement, particularly in the early stages before these plants have become established.

When the pool is to be surrounded with a wall, the shell should again be placed in the raised or half-raised position and bedded on sand. Walls in either brick or stone can be built around the perimeter, but allowing sufficient width from the edge to accommodate the paving if this is to be used (Fig 15). The walls should be constructed to finish at the same level as the pool. The cavity between the pool and the wall can be back-filled with sand; the coping will rest on the pool and wall and be cemented into place. Formal pools can be paved with concrete slabs but informal pools should be edged with crazy paving, preferably natural stone.

CONTAINERS AS WATER GARDENS
So far we have dealt with the more widely known and used types of water garden but, as

53

was pointed out earlier, lack of space or even lack of an orthodox garden is no bar to having something comparable. Even a bowl as small as 30cm (12in) in diameter and 15cm (6in) deep, placed near a sunny window, can become a miniature aquatic indoor garden complete with a miniature water-lily. Some loam in the bottom and a good light will make it a pleasing and unusual talking point.

Outside, wooden tubs, old wine and beer barrels and window-boxes, suitably lined, will easily adapt to this technique as will old-fashioned sinks. They may not look particularly elegant at first, but they will provide a most unusual and attractive feature when planted. Metal containers and fittings could prove fatal to plants, and especially fish; so before use paint them with a suitable rubber paint. Untreated copper can be particularly dangerous. Bear in mind that small receptacles are not suitable for anything other than minor displays. They will take a few plants but not the whole range, and it is extremely doubtful that fish could survive a winter out of doors.

This restriction does not apply to an indoor water display. Millions of people keep fish in glass tanks and you are merely extending the idea, though an indoor installation is a very specialised form of water gardening. Given a large enough room there is no reason whatever why some kind of liner should not be installed complete with plants, fish, lights, a fountain and even a watercourse.

There is the proviso that, to be really successful, this arrangement should be in a conservatory or in a room that offers plenty of natural daylight. If there is difficulty about this, modern technology can help to some extent in that whatever daylight is available can be supplemented by special lamps providing a full spectrum of light. The plants need as much sun and light as possible to flourish; the aim must therefore be to provide maximum light and the most natural atmosphere possible. In recent years thousands of householders have invested in room extensions and so have a kind of garden room between the house and the outdoors. This is an ideal situation to exploit.

Water, ever fascinating, takes on a new appeal in an indoor situation – you are never short of an interest. An indoor pool need never look lifeless, and enjoyment can be permanent for one can still watch it in comfort when the frosts come.

6 Stone for Edges and Features

EDGING STONES

The worst of the hard physical work of constructing the water garden may be over, but now you face the equally vital task of making it look good; indeed perfection here is vital. Small errors in excavating or measuring can usually be hidden by water and plants, but with the surround everything you do will be on display, and an error in preparation could mar the effect permanently. Conversely, a good job here can hide small blemishes in construction, so a little preliminary thought is needed, as well as care (even more than skill) in carrying out your ideas.

The edging is there only to camouflage the liner and other parts of 'the works' and make the pool look complete, but unless the work is done well the best that can be said is that the hoped-for natural effect will be lost.

To consider the sheet-liner type first; the liner is in position, and probably already full of water and settling down nicely. But you have some surplus inches of the sheet lying on the ground alongside, anchored temporarily by a few paving stones or other weights. For most people the instinctive solution will be to finish off by making a paved terrace all round the edge, especially with a formal design.

To do this, cut back the surplus sheeting so that you have only 10cm (4in) overlap all round (the offcuts may be useful elsewhere). Lay the stones carefully on the overlap in perfect alignment and, of course, absolutely level. A good under-layer of sand to act as a bed will eliminate most of the problems that arise from little pebbles that always seem to appear in the most awkward places when you are trying to get a perfect soil bed.

For all their intended artistic appearance, the prime reason for the paving slabs being there is a purely practical one – to keep the liner in place and out of sight. Although slabs 45cm (18in) square can be used, I would strongly recommend either 60cm (24in) square or 60cm x 45cm (24in x 18in), certainly for the row at the edge of the pool. Place the

Photo 13 Crazy paving using natural stone is the usual method of edging an informal pool

short 45cm (18in) side along the edge but also butting about 5cm (2in) over it. The chief reason for this is that most types of plastic sheet are at risk if exposed to the sun (butyl is the best-known exception), and this risk is greatest where the liner leaves the water and tucks under the edge. The protruding slabs will not only hide the liner but will also provide the necessary protection (see Photo 18).

The reason for putting the short side out is that there will be less risk of tipping should someone be standing right on the end; the extra weight on the land side will help to maintain the person's balance. The stones should, of course, be fixed and, while there is no real need to cement large slabs in position, it is a good idea to bed them into a dry mortar mix (3 parts sand to 1 part cement) and to brush in the same mixture between the joins. In due course the atmosphere will dampen the mixture and set it. Smaller slabs 30cm x 30cm (12in x 12in) or even 45cm x 45cm (18in x 18in) should be laid on mortar to ensure a firm and solid edge.

Unfortunately, life is not quite so uncomplicated as I have made it sound here. It is easy to work out designs for paving along straight edges, but formal pools can be round or have curved edges. In this case, slabs can be cut with a hammer and bolster (a special chisel about 5cm (2in) wide); alternatively paving can be laid on a radius and the triangular gaps filled with mortar. Crazy paving or bricks can also be used successfully for these pools.

For informal pools use crazy paving. Some people, shirking the time-consuming jigsaw game of sorting out the right bits to produce the most pleasing design, cement over the whole area and, before it sets, carve wriggly lines and shapes to simulate crazy paving. You often see paths made this way. Please don't do it. I did once, and have regretted it ever since! For a novel informal pool gaps can be left in the crazy paving and filled either by planting cushion plants such as thymes and saxifrages or by bedding in cobbles and smaller pebbles.

The effect can be quite pleasing.

I strongly recommend using natural stone as the crazy-paving edge to an informal pool; it should be 2·5cm to 5cm (1–2in) thick. It may be slightly more expensive than broken slabs but will blend in well for evermore so is well worth the difference. Depending on thickness, a tonne (ton) will cover approximately 10m² (12sq yd) or, put another way 50kg (1cwt) will give you about 1m (3½ft) of paving 45cm (18in) wide. As you get away from the edge of the pool, it will be enough to bed any paving stones on sand without using mortar. But as I have stressed, it is essential to make sure the actual edge next to the pool is fixed and solid (see Photo 13).

Another point to remember for future peace of mind when laying paving is to set it slightly below the level of any surrounding grass. Then, when you mow the lawn, the machine will run over the edge without causing or suffering any damage.

A rock edge to the pool offers an attractive alternative to paving (see Photo 14). The illustration clearly shows how effective it can be, but it will involve ordering a slightly larger liner because the planting ledge for marginal plants – normally 23cm (9in) – will have to be wider to accommodate the thickness of the stones (see Fig 8). Normally this extra will be 10–15cm (4–6in), but it would be as well to choose your stones before ordering the liner so that you know exactly how much you must allow.

Random rock creates a much more natural appearance. Fixing the stones is a straightforward operation: they are simply bedded into the 3–1 mortar mix of sand and cement, cushioned onto the liner. One great attraction of this method is that, within reason, the rocks

Page 57 (above) An ornamental bridge is a charming feature to include in the design for a water garden; *(below)* a large flat stone at the head of a waterfall ensures a dramatic fall of water

Photo 14 Rock stone offers a rugged edging for larger pools

Page 58 (above) Iris laevigata 'Colchesteri'; *(below)* an unusual poolside ornament lends added interest to this well-established pool

can be as big and as jagged as you like, so long as they have their bed of mortar underneath. That cushions the stone, and when the mortar sets the whole stone is supported evenly and no jagged edges will penetrate the liner. The liner should be pulled up at the back of the stones, taking care to cover jagged rocks with cement or offcuts of liner. It can then be trapped in position with soil and the surplus liner trimmed off. The surround can now be grassed or made into an alpine bed or similar.

So many types of edging are available that the choice is rather bewildering. The important thing is that whatever form you choose it must blend in with the surrounding landscape. Paving is the obvious choice for most situations, but you could have bricks or even cobbles. Bricks can be very slippery and cobbles are hard on the feet, but the effect can be pleasing, especially if you leave little gaps where ground cover plants can thrive and provide a little extra colour. A good use for cobbles in larger-scale operations is referred to below.

An alternative to stones or grass is to have a bog garden adjoining part of the pool, where you can grow plants whose roots must be damp but not waterlogged. Since a bog garden must always be very damp you must ensure that neither soil nor water can escape, and the soil level must be kept as high as possible. The way to do this is simply to extend your liner so that it spreads to whatever area you want, say a yard out from the pool edge, cover it with soil, and plant up. Again you will need rock stones cemented in place to form the boundary, the surplus liner being tucked up behind them and held in place with soil (see Fig 61).

Another alternative to consider is the grassed edge. This again can be very attractive, but care must be taken when mowing to keep the cuttings out of the water. With liner pools the edge will not be firm enough without support and will collapse. To get the necessary support, lay flat stones on edge and bed them into and against a bed of mortar mix. Trim the liner to the top of the stone, and now you can lay grass or have a flower-bed close to the water's edge (Fig 16).

If you have a large enough area you can get away from the conventional pool-side effect by additional excavating in the form of a horizontal arc, giving a half-saucer shape leading down to the water's edge. Again you will need to allow for extra liner, probably up to a yard all round, and you can fill this area with cobbles or small paving stones (Fig 17). This will provide a miniature beach effect as you approach the water. You will need to get a smooth line to the excavation, but the effect is pleasing and unusual. Bedding in the stones and cobbles is very simple: they are merely laid into a bed of mortar. For reasons of size, layout and, to be honest, skill, these grander schemes are more suitable for parks and public gardens than for private enjoyment, but they may provide an idea or two that can be adapted to a smaller-scale operation.

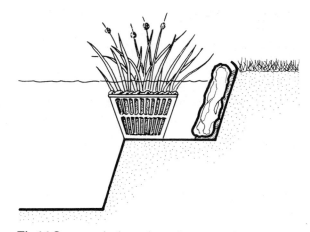

Fig 16 Grass can be brought to the water edge by supporting the liner with paving or rock laid as illustrated

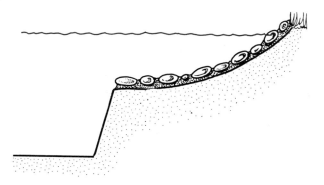

Fig 17 This edging has cobble stones laid on the liner

One of the best uses for cobbles is when you have what is known as a wildlife pool where ducks, geese etc are kept. While, normally, a cobble effect all round the perimeter of such a pool is not recommended there are places, notably in between areas where you are using a lot of rocks, where you can use them very effectively to make a 'beach'. Claws could easily put a sheet liner at risk as the birds come out of the water; cobbles, carefully bedded into a mortar mix, will protect the liner.

Before leaving the subject of edging, one must mention the marginal shelf, or ledge, for planting. All the edges shown assume that marginals will be planted in crates on the

Photo 15 Informal pool set at the bottom of a rockery showing the effect of large rock edging and cobbled edging

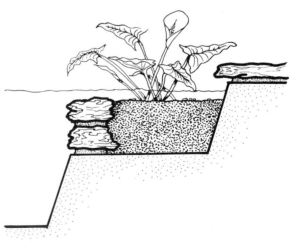

Fig 18 Construction for marginal planting pockets; the paved edging should be laid on mortar and should overlap the pool

61

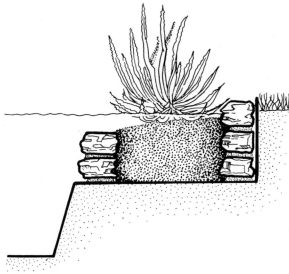

Fig 19 Construction for marginal planting pockets (stone edging)

ledge. But you can create a planting pocket by simply building up the marginal ledge with stone, leaving an area that can be filled with soil and planted (Figs 18 & 19). A problem with this method is that some plants will spread rapidly and choke less vigorous varieties, so take care when choosing your marginal plants – reference to the list in Chapter 12 may help your selection.

STEPPING-STONES AND ISLANDS

Another idea is to have a series of stepping-stones across the pool. These 'stones' are generally large blocks in the form of 30cm (12in) cubes, but they can go up to about 1m (3ft) cube and weigh up to 2 tonnes (tons) – reckon on 76kg per ·02m³ (1½cwt per cu ft). All that is necessary is to lay a large enough offcut of butyl or other suitable material on the base of the pool to form a mat or cushion. Provide a cement bed and set the stone or stones in place, so that you finish with something even and solid at or slightly above water level.

Now that we are going into the higher echelons of making a pool and 'ornamentation' you can, given the space and the incentive, be really imaginative and use your stepping-stones to get somewhere, such as an island out in the centre. Again, construction is very simple, but the effect can be good. All you need is another offcut of liner, the size of your proposed island. The stonework is cemented in to form a wall, and the area you have enclosed is then in-filled with soil to whatever height you want, and planted. Obviously, large pools are necessary for this effect.

7 Additional Construction Notes and the Koi Pool

So far we have been concerned only with installing the pool. But we cannot leave the subject of construction without paying attention to specific problems, and knowing what to do should anything go wrong. Construction is comparatively easy, but there are traps for the unwary.

DRAINING THE POOL

Occasional maintenance work – either tracing and curing a leak, or straightforward cleaning – becomes necessary with any type of pool, and this inevitably means emptying it, being careful to put any fish into a temporary tank while the work is in progress.

It might occur to some owners to install a drainage system so that the pool can be emptied like a bath, by pulling out a plug. But apart from the obvious difficulties of plugging a plastic liner to form a watertight seal over the hole, the drain would almost certainly choke up with dirt the first time it was used. (Special pools, to house Koi carp, have special needs, see page 66.)

In some circumstances it is possible to siphon out the water, but this depends on the level of the water compared with that of the lowest suitable draining position. In most cases the simplest way of emptying a pool is to use a pump. If you have a fountain or waterfall you can simply fit the garden hose on to the outlet and pump the water to the nearest drain. If not, there is a very cheap pump attachment for an electric drill that will do the job adequately. It can handle 910 litres (200gal) an hour and, although continuous running is not advised, it could empty a small pool.

There could be a case for allowing for an overflow, but even this is a rare requirement. For obvious reasons, the water level should be kept as high as possible, for on a hot day evaporation could easily cause a drop of 12mm (½in), and the smaller the pool surface the greater the comparative volume loss. A heavy storm, or a prolonged period of rain, might cause the pool to overflow; but normally this would be temporary and the surplus would soak away fairly quickly into the surrounding area. A 12mm or 19mm (½in or ¾in) tube could be bedded into the mortar under the pool edging to carry it a greater distance away.

FILLING THE POOL

Replenishment is more of a priority than drainage. It is unlikely the pool will ever need topping up in autumn, winter or spring, but, in summer evaporation can cause the water level to drop some 5cm (2in) or more in a week of very warm weather, particularly if there are also warm breezes. This loss can easily be replaced using the garden hose – in average British summers, this situation will arise only three or four times.

Automatic filling can be done by means of a normal household ball-valve as used in a toilet system. It is better if this is kept separate from the pool in a small plastic tank (cold-water cistern tanks are ideal), the water level in the tank being linked to that of the pool, using a special inlet fitting and length of tube. A suitable water supply is connected to the ball-

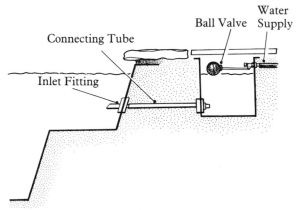

Fig 20 A simple method of automatically maintaining the water level in the pool

valve, adjustment of which will enable you to maintain the minimum water level exactly as required. All parts of the 'works' can be easily hidden away (Fig 20).

INLET FITTINGS

It might seem difficult to pass a tube through a liner and make a permanent seal, but the special inlet fittings already referred to give a watertight connection and can be used with any form of pool liner whether glass fibre, pre-formed, or flexible sheet. They are available in different sizes and come in two parts, one for each side of the liner. A hole is cut in the liner, the two parts are coated with a mastic seal and then screwed together, making a watertight joint. This device is also useful where you have two pools close together, for it will join them and maintain the same water level in each. It is also a simple way of ensuring gravity feed to a surface pump, indeed it can be used wherever tubing enters or leaves a pool.

CONSTRUCTION PROBLEMS

Frequent waterlogging is bound to occur where a pool has been built in a permanently damp or wet area, usually because the owner has ignored practical advice and considerations for the sake of an attractive position in a dell. Water forms below the pool and may lift

the flexible liner off the base of the excavation – in severe cases the liner may even rise to the surface. This situation can only be overcome by draining the area into a soakaway or ditch. Luckily, this task has been eased by the flexible drainage pipes now available, and which are very easy to lay. Always ensure that the fall is gradual, and always away from the area to be drained. Heavy storms can deliver an enormous amount of rain, so unless your soakaway is of adequate size you will have wasted your time.

Occasionally, even a properly constructed pool sited in the right place can suffer from waterlogging – a devastating sight for the poor owner who has worked so hard for perfection. It is far more likely to occur in a new pool or one under construction than in an established layout. Usually when it happens the pool is empty, or nearly so, for some reason, this coinciding with a period of heavy rain. One small consolation is that it is not due to a fault in construction, but a consequence of more or less freak weather conditions at the wrong time. It can largely be avoided by not emptying the pool in very wet periods.

A far more probable catastrophe is having the sides crumble when excavating. In most soils, the sides should be sloped at an angle of 20 degrees from vertical, but in very sandy soil this should be up to 45 degrees. If you are digging in a lawn, the soil will normally be firm and compact; but if you are using an area previously dug – a flower-bed or vegetable patch for example – it will be more crumbly. The best plan is to give the soil time to compact before starting to dig. Patience is needed!

Weeds are a widely ignored source of trouble, yet some have razor-sharp growing points that can penetrate not only pool liners, but even tarmac and concrete paths. Usually when a pool is excavated all weeds are removed, but not always, especially if in a sunken area or dip, or it is to be a raised pool. In these circumstances, or where there is heavy weed infestation, weed-killing is essential. Use a translocating type to kill the roots, being careful that none can leach into the pool when finished, as it would harm fish and plants.

Rodents can also damage pool liners, rats being the most likely culprits. One consolation is that this usually happens around the water-line, so is fairly easy to detect and repair. A magnifying glass will often show where the material has been gnawed. If rodents are the culprits you can either set traps or lay poison; but put the bait in an enclosed receptacle, such as a drainpipe, so that pets and wild birds are not exposed to danger.

LEAKS

If the water level of a pool drops, it is automatically assumed there is a leak. This is not necessarily so – evaporation in warm summer weather can reduce the level by 5cm to 8cm (2–3in) a week without there being a leak at all. Or a tube or hose leading from the pool may siphon out the water. It may even be that the pool edge is not level and the water is simply overflowing at the lowest point.

If you have a flexible liner, inspect any creases, particularly in the corners; it is possible the folds have slipped below water level, leading to an escape. If you have a waterfall, switch it off and watch the water level of the pool; if it remains constant the leak is in the waterfall, not in the pool.

Having checked all these points, if the water level continues to fall, it must be assumed that a leak has developed. Tracing this can be difficult and invariably the smaller the cause the harder it is to find and seal.

Concrete pools have their own peculiar problems; although they are not usually prone to accidental damage, they are vulnerable to frost damage and subsidence. Water will penetrate a hairline crack with a determination that has to be seen to be believed, and it is no consolation to the owner that in nine cases out of ten the fault is not his. In addition water will frequently seep away from a new concrete

pool – the drop can be quite dramatic. The difficulty here is that there are no apparent defects.

The cause is simple enough, and it may be some relief to discover that there is no fault in construction. For all its strength and solidity, concrete is very porous and is not easy to make waterproof. New pools can be made so by sealing with a proprietary paint, and this can also be applied to older structures that have developed a leak. As with all paintwork, the surfaces must be perfectly clean and defective areas repaired. If the concrete has perished, or there are large cracks, a flexible liner can be installed.

In liner pools, leaks may be due to insufficient care having been taken when installing the liner. If a sharp stone or flint is left in the excavation this may puncture the liner, but in this case the water level will usually drop within the first few days. If a liner begins to leak after a period of time, the cause may be more difficult to determine.

Liners can be damaged by children poking with a stick, or dogs clawing at them when trying to get out after a swim. Other more obscure causes like rodent attack and weeds have already been mentioned. One factor to consider is the age of the liner: polythene and some of the cheaper PVC sheets have only a limited life and it may be they have started to harden and split. To locate the source of the leak a careful examination of the liner is required. If this does not reveal the puncture then the water should be allowed to drain to its lowest level and the liner checked along the water-line. Care must be taken with the plants and fish. The marginal plants need only be lifted from the pool and kept well watered. The water-lilies and oxygenating plants must not be allowed to dry out and, if the water is going to drain below their level, they should be removed to a suitable container. The fish can remain in the pool to begin with, but if they begin to show signs of distress or if the water drops to a shallow level they should be removed and kept in aerated water (see Temporary Pools below). It is a great advantage to have a secondary pool if space permits; it can always be of interest and will be a useful emergency standby.

Glass-fibre pool liners are not so easily damaged, but can crack under the weight of the water unless properly bedded. This could be caused either by insufficient compaction when back-filling during construction or ground subsidence afterwards. Repair is quite easy using one of the proprietary repair kits, but give it ample time to harden as it may be toxic in its fluid state. Before refilling make certain the pool is adequately supported. Even a small pool of say $1 \cdot 8m^2$ (20sq ft) surface area will carry about $\cdot 7$ tonnes (¾ ton) of water.

TREATING CONCRETE

Untreated concrete is toxic to fish, due to the effect on the pH of the water as described in Chapters 16 and 17. Concrete pools can be neutralised using a curing agent, or by coating with a specialised paint. However, there is a problem with paving surrounds resting on mortar, or anywhere where mortar is used in the pool. It is not practical to cure this, so scrub and rinse the area with clear water or, better still, with a solution of potassium permanganate – available from a chemist.

If mortar is used in the pool, for instance in an internal wall or under stepping-stones or rocks, crystals of potassium permanganate should be dissolved in the water until a deep-purple coloration is obtained. After a few days the pool should be emptied, scrubbed out and refilled.

TEMPORARY POOLS

These are very useful as a temporary home for fish and plants when emptying the pool. They should be erected indoors – a garage or shed is ideal – where they will be out of direct sunlight and away from cats and other predators. A small air pump should provide adequate aeration for fish for a few days.

Children's paddling pools make excellent temporary pools, or one can easily be made with four planks of wood nailed at the corners and lined with polythene. Fasten the sheet to the top edge using staples or drawing pins, and remember to place weights against the planks for extra support.

KOI-POOL CONSTRUCTION

Until now we have concentrated on pools where the interdependence of plants, fish and waterfalls is used to enhance a landscape and form a garden in the water. Koi pools are different, for although a waterfall or even a fountain may be included there will be no plants – simply water and fish. There are many excellent books dealing specifically with this hobby and there are many Koi societies worldwide. The Koi keeper, with his single-minded objective, will need the detailed information which these provide; but the basic principles of Koi-pool construction are explained here (Fig 21).

The whole concept differs. A water garden will blend with its surroundings, but a Koi pond presents difficulties here because the water itself is bare. This can be overcome to a certain extent by clever planting at the edges, but you are unlikely to integrate it so easily into the landscape as with a water garden.

Koi pools are $1 \cdot 2m$ (4ft) or more in depth and, as there are few prefabricated pools of sufficient dimension, construction will be of a liner material or concrete. Concrete requires shuttering, a knowledge of construction techniques and many strong helping hands, so most pools are made with a liner. Not that construction with a liner is as straightforward as previously described. Because of the depth the sides have to be supported. This entails building walls of concrete blocks and then fitting the pool liner.

In addition a bottom drain is required to get rid of the mulm (sediment) and fish waste products that accumulate on the floor. We advised against a drain in the water-garden construction, because it would be rarely

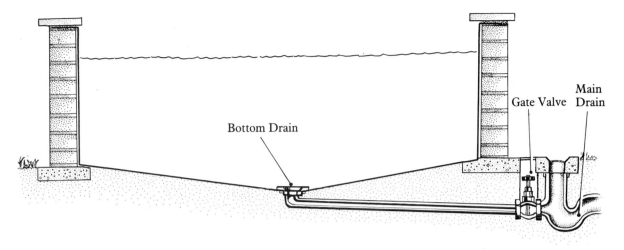

Fig 21 A typical construction for a Koi pool showing the bottom drain, concrete blocks at the side and the flexible pool liner

needed and the build-up of mud and debris in the water would be likely to clog it the first time it was used. However, with a Koi pool the bottom drain is in frequent use and, as there are no plants or soil, the build-up of mud is insignificant and the water is able to carry this away without fear of clogging. The drain is closed by a gate-valve, which is opened periodically to allow water and sediment to flow away to a convenient point. It is fitted in the lowest part of the pool and the base is sloped to carry the mulm and waste to it.

The water level should be approximately 23cm (9in) below the pool walls to deter cats and birds, and to stop fish jumping out of the pool. As there is no plant life, the pool will require a complete filtration system (see Chapter 11) and provision must be made for pipework between pool and filter.

Shade must also be considered, as there will be none of the plant life which naturally affords this cover in a conventional pool.

8 Equipping the Pool

PUMPS AND THEIR FUNCTIONS

With the structural work completed, you can now get on with the enjoyable task of bringing your pool to life. Many owners are content to fill their pool with water, stock it with plants and fish, and leave it at that. There is nothing wrong with this, but to stop here may result in the water garden failing to reach its full potential. The water remains still, save for any movement generated by fish, though the presence of plants will prevent it from becoming stagnant – a fear that may well have put some people off the idea of having a water feature of any kind in the garden. To make your pool really come to life you must get the water moving; this inevitably means installing a pump. The range of types, sizes and capacities available may seem confusing, but at least it is so comprehensive that you are virtually guaranteed to find one tailor-made for your needs.

Curiously, there is a widespread misconception concerning the movement of water. Many people – and I was once among them – believe that if you want a continuous flow of water it must come from a tap. This is completely wrong; in spite of the growth in sales of pools and equipment in recent years which has put this fallacy largely in its place, even today you find unenlightened people complaining about 'the waste of water' if public fountains are left running when a few days of hot dry summer weather bring the inevitable drought warnings. Nowadays, most fountains and man-made waterfalls are operated by a pump and waste no water. The entire volume is recirculated by the pump; nothing runs away down a drain, and a running supply is unnecessary.

A pump will be the basis for extending your interests and will prove one of your best gardening investments. Even if you originally baulk at the cost because of uncertainty about the type and capacity you require, you have a literally watertight guarantee against making the wrong choice since most suppliers will willingly exchange your newly bought pump for a larger one if you find when you start it up that it is inadequate for your purpose. Should you still be unconvinced of the enormous extra pleasure you will get as the result of installing a fountain and/or waterfall, there is one technical point that should sweep away all opposition. Pleasing though they are to eye and ear, fountains and waterfalls are not just for ornamentation. They have a definite function, especially in hot humid conditions when the oxygen level in the water falls quite dramatically. Continuously moving water remedies this defect, not only offering a visual attraction but also introducing fresh oxygen.

Possibly some people refrain from investigating the benefits of moving water because they think a pump is a complicated piece of apparatus. If there are any complications, they are purely in the manufacture and do not affect the purchaser. Certainly there are few, if any, in its use. Ignoring the technical jargon that surrounds most forms of mechanism, basically a pump is a specially designed casing (the pump body) with an inlet for water to be drawn in and an outlet to let it out. Inside the casing is a paddle (the impeller) which rotates to eject water through the outlet, this water being replaced by the water being drawn in, thus maintaining a continuous flow (Fig 22).

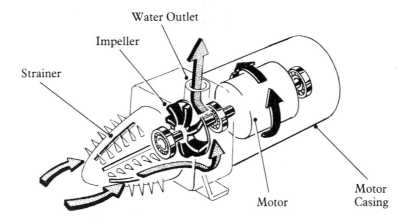

Fig 22 A pump simply draws in water through the inlet and ejects it under pressure through the outlet

The dictionary defines a pump as a device for raising or moving water by suction and omits to mention that it is generally worked by some form of motor. The pumps we shall be discussing are all operated by a small electric motor which is built into the casing; thus pump and motor are integral and supplied in one unit.

A pump installed in a water garden will be required to operate either a fountain, a water-

Fig 23 A typical low-voltage installation with the transformer housed under cover

fall, or a filtration unit, or a combination of any of these. Broadly there are two types of pump – submersible, which operate in the pool, under water; and surface, which are housed separately on dry land as near (but also as inconspicuously) as possible to the water area. Both types demand a certain amount of thought before you buy, for there are pros and cons concerning each. The submersibles are probably more convenient for most owners, and certainly more of this type are sold, so I will deal with these first.

SUBMERSIBLE PUMPS
Submersibles, as the name implies, are designed to operate completely submerged,

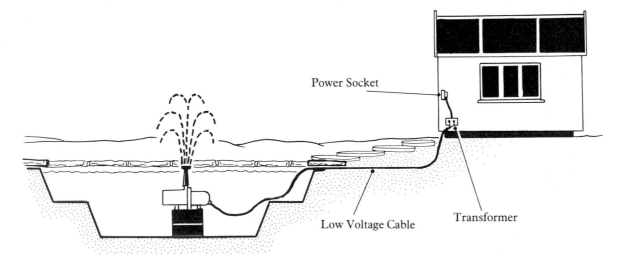

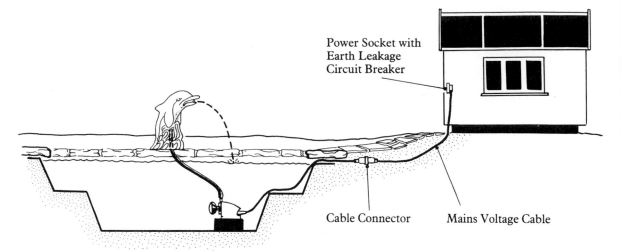

Power Socket with
Earth Leakage
Circuit Breaker

Cable Connector   Mains Voltage Cable

Fig 24 The mains-voltage pump connected to the nearest earthed electrical supply; the fountain ornaments are operated by the pump at the side of the pool

though a few can also work in a dry situation. They are all electrically powered, but offer a choice of voltage. Mains types are simply connected direct to the mains supply; the low-voltage ones come with a small transformer, which must be housed in a garage or shed or some other shelter away from the pump but near the mains supply point (Fig 23). The transformer reduces the normal 240V down to 24V in Britain; similar transformers in the USA reduce mains voltages of 115 down to 24. (For lighting systems, transformers usually reduce to 12V.) I stress that the transformer must be sited between the mains socket and the apparatus; thus the cable between the transformer and pump carries only the low voltage and is therefore completely safe. Although I would not advise handling a live terminal under water, even if the cable were cut or damaged no serious injury should be caused to anyone touching it. Transformers have done a lot to remove doubts about the wisdom of using electricity in the damp or wet conditions that go with any form of gardening, but you must still show respect for it. The cost of a low-voltage pump and transformer is very

similar to that of a mains-voltage type. Unfortunately only the smaller-performance pumps are available in low voltage.

Submersible pumps, whether mains or low voltage, have a length of cable sealed into the unit. If, as frequently happens, this length is not enough for your needs, an extension cable can easily be fitted, but you must take adequate precautions by joining the lengths of cable with a waterproof or weatherproof connector. For permanent installations you must comply with the local Electricity Board and Institute of Electrical Engineers (IEE) regulations in Britain or Institute of Electrical and Electronics Engineers (IEEE) in the United States or the strict regulations of the various state electricity boards in Australia.

One great advantage submersibles have over surface pumps is that the installation is so simple. Little or no plumbing is required: you merely place the pump in the pool in a convenient spot with whatever attachment you need to operate fountain or waterfall, and switch on (Fig 24). You can even mount the fountain jet onto the pump if you wish. The important point is that it must be completely submerged, which doubtless partly accounts for the astonishing quietness of these appliances.

Although, understandably, low-voltage

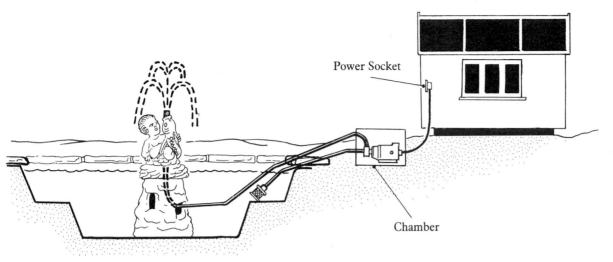

Power Socket

Chamber

Fig 25 Surface pump installation showing the pump housed in a separate chamber

submersibles are regarded as the safest types, the safety factor is by no means overlooked with the mains versions, whether submersible or surface, for it is now possible to fit a device that cuts off the current virtually immediately anything goes wrong. Earth Leakage Circuit Breakers (ELCB) have been around for a long time, but they are expensive and require expert installation. Nowadays, however, a simple version is on the market, called, appropriately, Power Breaker. It can be fitted to any appliance using normal mains voltage and, should any fault develop such as a frayed or cut cable, the breaker trips and cuts off the power in less time than it takes to blink and before any injury can occur.

SURFACE PUMPS

Surface pumps are generally fed directly from the mains, but they can be used with the Power Breaker. They are not normally supplied with any cable and must be housed in a dry, watertight and well-ventilated chamber as near as possible to the pool (Fig 25). It is usual to turn this situation to advantage by installing a power socket in the chamber; it is then a simple matter to connect the pump to the mains supply. Again permanent installations must be in accordance with local Electricity Board regulations and, while you are about it, it is advisable to put in a multi-point socket at very little extra cost. You can then run pump, waterfall, fountain and lighting, or any other garden machinery (mower, hedge-trimmer, cultivator etc) provided the cable capacity is not exceeded.

Surface pumps offer a choice between those with induction motors and those with series-wound commutator motors. Induction types (the majority) can be run continuously over long periods. Do not buy a pump with a series-wound commutator motor unless you plan to use it only for very short periods; they are not usually suitable for continuous running. If you anticipate running for more than four hours at a time – and that period goes very quickly on a pleasant summer afternoon or evening – you need the induction type.

Generally, surface pumps, particularly the induction type, have a longer life than submersibles if correctly installed. In addition they usually develop more pressure and are able to operate higher fountains and waterfalls. Points against surface pumps are that they need a separate waterproof chamber, the smaller versions are more expensive than comparable submersibles, more fittings are

71

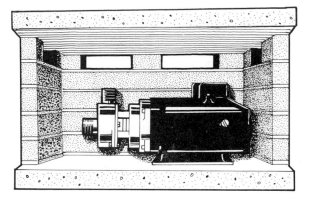

Fig 26 A surface pump chamber showing ventilation holes

required, and they can in some installations be noisy. Surface pumps need a heavy-duty inlet hose (as short as possible) to draw water from the pool, and an outlet tube to deliver it to the fountain or waterfall head. This can be any reasonable length but there is a 'friction factor', meaning that the volume of water at the point of ejection will be reduced on long distances.

If you decide on a surface pump you must pay careful attention to where it is housed. It must be fairly close to the pool because it is important to keep the suction tube as short as possible. The pump must be kept dry: usually it is housed in a brick-built chamber or box (Fig 26). A good solid concrete floor on which it can stand is recommended as a means of preventing moisture reaching it from the ground, and of course the chamber must be sited where there is no risk of flooding or seepage. Don't forget to fit a rainproof lid! There is another important factor when constructing the chamber. Many surface pumps get very hot when in operation and good ventilation is essential, not only to cool the motor but also to avoid condensation when the pump is switched off.

Lifting water above its natural level is the main function of all pumps used in water gardens, and a vital piece of information you must

have when purchasing a surface pump is what is called the 'maximum suction lift' (see Fig 27). In everyday terms, this is the vertical distance from the pool water level to the pump. The maximum suction lift is an important factor, for on this depends the success of your entire installation. If, for instance, you buy a pump with a 3m (10ft) msl, you must site it at a maximum of 3m (10ft) above the pool water level. At 3·3m (11ft) up it won't work, but at 3m (10ft) or less it will happily raise the water. Most pumps will draw water up to 3m (10ft); the large ones can draw it far higher.

Most surface pumps are not self-priming, which means that the suction tube must be filled with water before it can operate. Obviously, if it is sited above the pool water level the water will drain back whenever the pump is switched off, so repriming (refilling with water) will be necessary. There is, however, a simple way of avoiding this cumbersome operation – by fitting a foot-valve (see Fig 27). This allows water to pass only one way. It will be drawn from the pool to the pump, but when this is switched off it will prevent water passing back into the pool. After the initial priming when the pump is first installed, there is no need to worry about it again until the

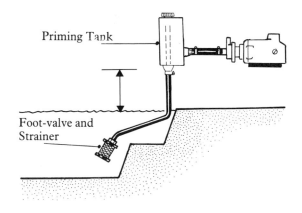

Fig 27 The 'suction lift' is the vertical distance between water level and the surface pump; to retain water and allow the pump to prime automatically a priming tank or foot-valve and strainer is used

apparatus is dismantled for winter storage or cleaning, or when the layout is changed.

There is an alternative method: a priming tank can be fitted to the pump inlet, and this retains enough water to allow the pump to prime automatically (Fig 27). Simpler still, if it is feasible, is to site the pump below the level of the water surface. The water will then feed naturally by gravity to the pump and a foot-valve will not be needed (Fig 28); but remember to avoid risk of flooding.

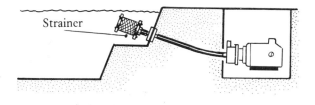

Fig 28 In this installation the water is fed by gravity to the pump

One piece of apparatus essential to all these operations is a strainer, the main function of which is to prevent leaves and debris interfering with the works. It is housed in the pool, fixed to the end of the suction tube, and of course must be cleared of debris from time to time. Normally this is a very simple task taking only a moment or two, and is made easier if the strainer is within easy reach from the side. Strainers are available which include an integral foot-valve, or the two items can be purchased separately.

SELECTION AND INSTALLATION
You will now realise why the choice of pump requires much thought and why many suppliers, recognising the difficulties of selection, offer an exchange service should you find you have underestimated the capacity you need. But what do we need to consider when selecting a pump?

By now you will probably have decided between a surface or submersible and whether

low or mains voltage. One pleasing tendency nowadays is that the guarantee periods tend to be longer. They all used to be one year, but now many manufacturers are giving two years, and this could sway your decision. Ask about spares, what they cost and if they are readily available. Ask, too, if the pumps are repairable. Many are sealed units, and if these go wrong or the cable frays it means buying a new pump. Another important point is the power consumption. Some pumps are designed with low-wattage motors which reduce operating costs and this is worth consideration, particularly where the pump is to be run for long periods.

I know that great confusion exists among newcomers concerning the types, size and function of pumps; but the important consideration is not so much the pump as what it is supposed to do. Fountains and waterfalls are somewhat opposite in their demands here. A fountain requires pressure; volume output is largely unnoticed. A waterfall needs volume above all else; and once water is carried to the top, gravity will provide the desired effect. As a dramatic illustration of this difference, a pump capable of delivering 1,818 lph (400gph) at a 1m (3ft) head may produce only 682 lph (150gph) through a fountain. The small holes in the fountain jet drastically reduce the output because of friction.

A common mistake is to site a submersible pump, or the tubing from a surface pump, right at the bottom of the pool. In such a position it must draw in mud and sediment, which will cloud the water and clog the strainer. It should rest on a block, clear of the sediment that is bound to form. You have to strike a happy medium: if you place it too close to the surface, not only is it likely to be seen more easily, it will also draw in the floating plants (Fig 29).

If a fountain only is required, choosing the correct size of pump is a simple matter; by now you should have settled whether you also want a fountain ornament (see Chapter 10).

73

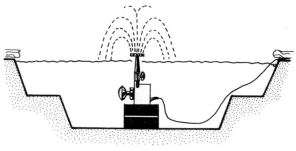

Fig 29 A submersible pump should be positioned so that it does not draw mud from the bottom or floating plants from the surface

Fig 30 Small fountains have the jet and flow adjuster mounted directly on the pump; the jet is installed slightly above water level

For a fountain, decide on the height and spread you require. With smaller fountain layouts the jet is often mounted directly on top of the pump, and normally a flow adjuster or gate-valve is also provided to control the height of the jet (Fig 30). For ornaments and larger fountains the pump is positioned at the side of the pool, and the water is carried to the fountain by tubing (see Fig 24).

Always consider the size of pool. Use a cane or pole to gauge the height of the fountain required, and bear in mind that the spray must return within the confines of the pool; you don't want it falling on the paving and surrounding area. In addition, if you are growing water-lilies the fountain spray must be kept away from them. Knowing the height of the jet, it is very easy to select a pump. Most manufacturers state the height of fountain each pump will service, and a specialist water-garden catalogue is all you need to help you decide.

Choosing the pump for a waterfall is slightly more difficult. With a watercourse, the width of the channel and how to fill it adequately must be taken into consideration. What may look a miniature torrent in a channel 5cm (2in) wide may be only a very thin sheet spread across 15 or 20cm (6 or 8in). Choosing the right pump thus becomes something of a guessing game if you want to get the right flow effect over the falls. For most purposes a fairly

lively flow will look best, and the general rule is to allow 227 litres (50gal) per hour for every 2·5cm (1in) width of waterfall. Thus a 15cm (6in) width will need a pump capable of delivering 1,362 lph (300gph) at the output head (height of waterfall).

Remember that too much turbulence will have a detrimental effect on the water-lilies and other submerged flowering plants. If the natural pool balance is not to be disturbed, the flow rate per hour should not exceed the pool volume. Thus a pool holding 910 litres (200gal) will have a maximum flow rate of 910 lph (200gph). A good way to gauge the flow required is to use the hosepipe as described for waterfalls on page 88. This will give a good idea what a given output of water will actually look like. Armed with this information, you are in a position to reach for a catalogue, compare pump performances and select one that suits your requirements.

When studying catalogues you will soon meet the technical term 'head' – the vertical distance between the surface of the pool and the point of discharge at the top of the waterfall (Fig 31). The depth of water in the pool does not have to be considered. Obviously, the

Page 75 (above) A mixed community of Koi carp; *(below)* feeding time for the Koi

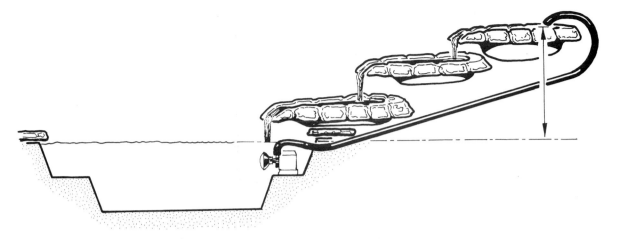

Fig 31 The 'head' is the height of the outlet above water level; the pump for a waterfall should be placed in the most convenient position near the return to the pool

higher the head the less water the pump will deliver. The maximum head may also be shown, and this is the height beyond which the pump ceases to pump any water. (The maximum head is not the height of fountain which the pump will operate.)

With so many types of pump on the market (and new ones appearing frequently), it is futile to attempt to analyse each one here. However, it may be helpful to explain a performance chart, an example of which is shown on page 78. This shows the make or model of pump on the left and across the top is the 'head' with the maximum head on the extreme right. The output of each pump can be read against the head; for example Pump 2 in the chart will give an output of 1,500 litres (330gal) per hour at ·9m (3ft), but will give only 795 litres (175gal) per hour at 2·1m (7ft). The examples are actual quoted figures.

This simple chart shows very clearly how increasing the head height drastically reduces output and how vital it is to get a pump large

Page 76 Iris kaempferi and *Scirpus albescens* by the water-side

enough for the job. Some manufacturers issue graphs showing the height and output of various models, and these details can also help in making your choice.

One thing the figures may not tell you is that they are maximum theoretical performance. They do not allow for frictional loss – the 'voltage drop' equivalent caused by friction due to the length and bore size of tubing passing a sharp bend or similar obstacle. Tees and gate-valves (which adjust flow and height) are other items that affect the theoretical performance. You can reduce this loss by using an adequate size of tubing (see page 88).

For a waterfall, the pump should be situated close to the water outlet, that is, near the bottom of the fall, so that the pump tubing can return the water to the head by the shortest route (see Fig 31). There is a widely held belief that the pump should be sited at the far end of the pool from the fall, to ensure that the water circulates properly. There is no need for this; water will always circulate naturally, moved by wind and fish. Keeping the pump at the far end merely increases the length of tubing required, and this in turn reduces the pump output. With a large pump, it could also create a current that would cause disturbance to the water-lilies.

The combined fountain and waterfall is easily achieved, given the right size of pump and a tee-piece. If you plan to have both a

PERFORMANCE CHART

	·9m	1·5m	2·1m	3·0m	4·2m	6·1m	Maximum head
			Head in metres				*Maximum*
Pump 1	910	545					1·8m
Pump 2	1,500	1,160	795				2·4m
Pump 3	1,910	1,770	1,590	1,365	570		4·8m
Pump 4	10,000	9,090	8,365	7,000	5,455	2,730	9·1m

	3ft	5ft	7ft	10ft	14ft	20ft	Maximum head
			Head in feet				*Maximum*
Pump 1	200	120					6ft
Pump 2	330	255	175				8ft
Pump 3	420	390	350	300	125		16ft
Pump 4	2,200	2,000	1,840	1,540	1,200	600	30ft

fountain and waterfall, base most of your calculations concerning pump size on the needs of the waterfall. Usually with the smaller type of unit a tee-piece fits between the pump and the fountain jet, giving two outlets. Tubing fitted to the tee-piece carries the water to the waterfall head, and fountain and waterfall can operate simultaneously. A flow adjuster included with the unit will control the fountain height (Fig 32). With larger layouts the pump is usually sited at the side of the pool and the water is carried to both fountain and waterfall through plastic tubing (Fig 33). Surface-pump layout is similar, except, of course, that the pump is mounted outside the pool (Fig 34).

I have devoted much space to the selection of the pump because it is essential to get the right one for the job. Study carefully what you want to achieve and the size and type of pump that will best suit your needs.

Choose the pump before you put in the pipework. I have heard of cases where enthusiasts built their waterfall, installed the equipment, and left buying the pump until last – and then found that the piping was wrong. Wrong-sized or otherwise inadequate tube had to be dug out and replaced. Bear in mind, too, that soft-walled tubes, though suitable for delivery, are useless on the suction side of a surface pump: they would collapse under the suction pressure.

Tees or crosses can be fitted into the outlet side of the pump to feed multiple fountains or waterfalls if you have the capacity, and you can have gate-valves to control flow and height. These usually have a screw fitting, which simplifies assembly and means the whole system can be set up without any expert plumbing knowledge (Fig 35).

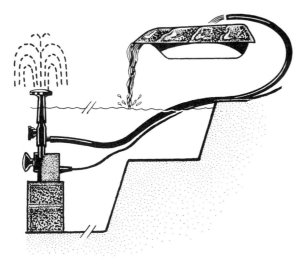

Fig 32 For small fountain and waterfall installations a tee-piece fits between the pump and jet

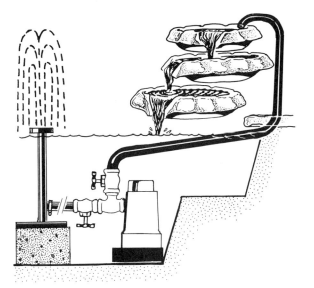

Fig 33 A large waterfall and a fountain can be operated from a larger submersible pump sited at the side of the pool

Fig 34 A typical fountain and waterfall layout operated from a surface pump

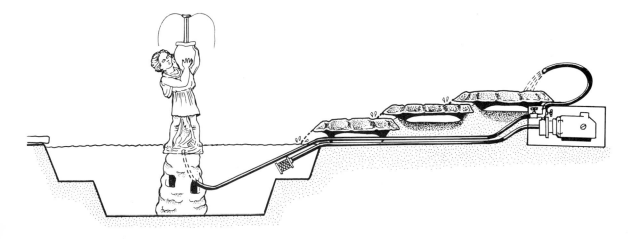

Remember to keep tube lengths short and as straight as possible to reduce friction loss to the minimum. That way you will achieve greater output and efficiency from your pump and, consequently, maximum pleasure from the sight and sound of moving water.

Before we leave this section, mention must be made of pools on different levels, linked with a waterfall. You may want to site the pump in the lower pool and have a fountain in

79

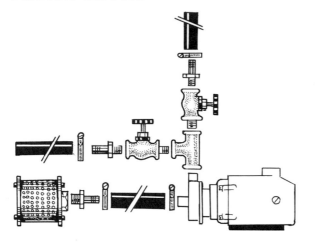

Fig 35 Pump fittings, including gate-valves, hose unions and tees, usually have screw threads for ease of assembly

the upper pool, the theory being that the fountain will provide the water for the waterfall. In practice this is rarely satisfactory as the small fountain holes drastically reduce the output of water. For this type of installation you should have a tee-piece (either on the pump or in the top pool): one feed from the tee will provide the water for the fountain and the other will discharge water directly into the upper pool to feed the waterfall.

9 Waterfalls

GENERAL CONSIDERATIONS

Unlike the orthodox garden, where there is always some job that needs to be done, you can relax completely beside your water garden, watching the fish and listening to the water as it splashes down the watercourse. Not many gardens have a natural spring or stream that can be incorporated into a water garden and, even if there is one, the blessings are mixed. The water is usually so cool that it inhibits the growth and flowering of plants, particularly water-lilies. Also, natural water can easily become polluted, affecting both plants and fish. A waterfall can easily be linked to a natural stream and water recirculated, but it is wiser to keep it as an independent system.

If you want an 'artificial' flow, water running from a tap must be ruled out; not only is it wasteful, it is cold, and the chlorine and other chemicals it contains are certainly detrimental to life in the pool. On all counts, therefore, a 'closed circuit' supply with a recirculating pump is the best answer.

Admittedly, building a watercourse is likely to be a bigger task than installing a fountain, but it is not so complicated as it may seem. In fact, you will probably be surprised, when you have done it, how easy it was. It is not necessary to have a number of high vertical steps – two or three 15cm (6in) 'risers' will produce a very satisfactory effect. Impressive though a long fall of water may look, you need go no higher than 1m (3ft) above the level of the pool. This is the ideal height for the average layout and for a gradual rock-outcrop effect centred on a small pool, and can be landscaped quite easily into the surroundings. There is nothing to prevent you from raising the level higher, particularly on a sloping site, but the overall effect must be in proportion to the pool and surrounding area.

If your pool is formal in design – circular, square, rectangular or L-shaped – a waterfall should not be installed unless it, too, is formal, with formal weirs and straight-sided channels. The laughing, dancing, will-of-the-wisp effect that makes a watercourse so enchanting must be confined to the informal layout if it is not to look incongruous.

It must be acknowledged that a waterfall is not essential to the balance of a pool; plants and fish can thrive without the benefit of moving water. Nevertheless, a waterfall – or a fountain, which produces a very similar effect – does have one definite benefit in that it introduces fresh oxygen into the water. This is a particular asset in hot sultry weather. In daytime plants absorb carbon dioxide and give off oxygen, but after dusk this process is reversed so that throughout the night the oxygen content of the water is gradually reduced and can be severely depleted by dawn. After a hot day, when high temperatures have already reduced the oxygen level, this situation can become critical; and in these conditions the wise owner, with thought for his fish, will keep waterfall or fountain running all night. A further benefit is that a waterfall operated continuously will provide to a small extent a biological filter, with beneficial bacteria forming on all surfaces helping to prevent the formation of algae.

There are various ways of constructing a waterfall, either by setting out prefabricated

Photo 16 Unusual tiered raised pool with linking waterfalls showing a formal weir effect

units or by a build-as-you-go system using concrete or waterproof sheet liner. The pre-fabricated-unit construction is limited to the shape, size and design of the units available. The design therefore needs careful thought. Ideally the vertical steps between units should not be more than 15cm (6in); if greater than this, care must be taken in positioning the units to avoid any chance of water loss. Never-theless, such units do have a great advantage over the other types because of the ease and speed with which they can be put into position ready for use.

In situ construction using a liner is likely to be much more satisfactory in the long run. It will take a lot more time and effort, but the result will be more rewarding and professional looking. You have much greater scope in the design, which can follow your own exclusive ideas. You can have a header pool, channels and waterfalls to any length and width, and you can site them exactly where you want them. Not for you a factory-made waterfall if you want this freedom to make your feature individual in every sense. Each waterfall can be separately designed and executed, giving an effect of rapids and weirs, or of sheer cas-cading water. Careful positioning of rocks and stone will provide you with many types of fall and varying sound.

Whichever type you use, prefabricated, concrete, or liner, it will have to be positioned in a mound of soil or bank which normally will be the excavations from the pool. There is, of course nothing to stop you going higher than this (if you don't mind the expense), and importing some rubble and more soil to give you all the scope you need. Naturally, you will have saved yourself work by planning where the waterfall is to be before excavating for the pool, so that the mound of soil is in the right place and approximately the right shape before you begin to build. Almost inevitably, that part of it not used for the actual channel will become a rockery.

One point to remember is that, when the waterfall is in operation, the water level will rise above the pouring lip and this must be taken into account when setting the edges.

CONSTRUCTION

It must be said for the prefabricated types of waterfall that they do make life easy. Though you have to accept the length, width, colour and outline in which they are made, they offer a good range and are easy to install. You can have a header pool, a large or small waterfall, a stream and a cascade in either single or multiple versions. They are all designed to fit together with an overlap, so you can have a combination of any of these. As with the prefabricated pools, they are available in either glass fibre or in heavy-duty semi-rigid plastic costing approximately half the price.

You will have to dig out a channel to take these units, but their shape and size will provide an easy guide to direction. Two points have to be borne in mind. A pool or cascade where water will lie must be sited absolutely level at the sides or the effect will be ludicrous, and as with constructing the basic pool you will have to make sure that the units are firmly bedded. A good cushioning layer of sand and well-compacted back-filling will accomplish this. The principle is exactly the same as when setting a preformed pool, but the work is not so arduous.

The glass-fibre units are made to resemble natural stone. They do blend quite well with natural stone in a rockery, and are quite rigid. Semi-rigid plastic units will not be so satisfactory. Being less rigid, they are a little more difficult to install; they need more firming to ensure that they are properly levelled, otherwise they tend to flex and the water runs over the side. The main disadvantage of the plastic

types is that they are more affected by ultra-violet light. With pools, most of the material is under water and gets some protection, but in the watercourse much of it is exposed and at the mercy of ultra-violet rays. Their life expectancy is therefore considerably less. One further point is that they are not so natural looking; but as they are much cheaper than glass-fibre or concrete units they are a popular buy, especially if it is intended that the watercourse is not to remain in place indefinitely (dare I suggest thoughts of an improved and enlarged version after a few years?).

There is another kind of preformed unit, made from precast concrete. These are comparatively expensive, rather bulky, and are heavy to transport and install, but they should give long service. Being individual units, they are less vulnerable than normal concrete to the effects of earth settlement. They have quite a natural appearance but, because they are concrete, lime will wash into the pool and affect the water. Most of the units currently available have not been cured, so should be treated as detailed in Chapter 7.

All preformed waterfall units are relatively easy to camouflage by careful planting using creeping varieties which will soon cover the edges of the units. One very important point that needs to be watched for the first few months (even the first few years) is that, because your rockery will have been freshly constructed, there will be some earth settlement. This could cause prefabricated units to tilt and result in some spillage, and consequent water loss, over the side. Rate and frequency of settlement will depend on a number of factors, not only soil type; but when it happens it is usually a fairly simple matter to level the units again.

The purely do-it-yourself approach to a waterfall, where you are using a sheet liner or concrete, does call for considerably more thought when planning. The key here is to think of the falls as steps linking two levels in the garden, and I cannot do better than quote

Photo 17 Flat stones on a waterfall provide a weir effect

the method adopted by one of the most experienced and imaginative landscape designers in the country:

Having the mound of soil where I want to create the waterfall, I look at it as though I'm constructing a path through a rising garden. I draw a line meandering and bending through the mound to create an interesting path. Then I gradually cut back the soil, forming the path to whatever width I want, and creating the steps as I rise up the bank.

If I want a deep weir type of fall I will cut further back into the bank to create a deeper step for the weir effect, and make shallower steps where I need only a small ripple type of cascade. Working back from

the pool through the mound will create an interesting course with angles that form the waterfall through the rockery.

Note the point about angles and bends. They are more natural, and will improve the appearance and interest enormously compared with a straight fall.

With the design plan settled, the outstanding question is the type of liner, and as with other items of equipment there are some pros and cons to consider. Watercourses lined with butyl or PVC offer the greatest flexibility in design and construction, and when properly made have an almost unlimited life. Butyl is the most suitable, being the most flexible, but on a short-term basis you can use PVC quite successfully.

With the sheet method the liner acts simply as a flexible waterproof membrane covering the excavation or the path and steps down the watercourse. With the liner in place, a cement mix is laid on top, into which the stones are bedded. Once the liner is in place no water can escape; the stones are merely positioned to camouflage and build up the sides and falls to create an appearance as natural as possible. Basically, the task involves placing flat stone (preferably) or cobbles on the base of the stream and using rock stones round them. Rock stones are then built up along the side. The soil will hold the liner tight up against these rocks (Figs 36, 37, 38 & 39).

The method of building up the watercourse is clearly shown in the illustrations, but here are a few points to help you plan the work. First, cut out the watercourse and steps and any pools you wish to incorporate. Provided you don't go above the maximum 'head' – the lifting capacity of your pump – you can make the watercourse meander like a stream for any distance you like back down to the pool. Measure the length of liner required as you would a stair carpet. Allow extra material at each fall to form a pleat. This will give an amount of slack material which will be useful when the edges are lifted to form the channel. The width of the watercourse plus the depth at each side will give the width of liner required.

The liner can usually be supplied to the size required in a single sheet, or you can use two or more pieces if this is more convenient. This can be more economical when you have channels of varying width. When more than one liner is used the overlap must be arranged to coincide with a fall, making sure that the lower liner is higher than the water level in the channel (Fig 40).

You will find it easier to start at the base, at pool level, covering the water channel and ensuring that the sides are lined well above the proposed level of the water. The waterfall liner does not require joining to the pool liner; it is simply overlapped into the water. Set the stones to hold the liner in place as you work your way up.

At each fall set the stones on the face slightly higher, to retain water in the channel when the pump is switched off. Arrange the layout to include a number of little falls and a trough in between, which will retain the water. This can be done by sloping the channel (Fig 41), or by raising the liner at each fall using a brick or slab underneath (Fig 42). The presence of the water will still make the layout look quite attractive even when the pump is not operating.

The arrangement of stones on the face will determine the type of fall. Flat stones placed horizontally, with an overhang of 5 to 8cm (2 to 3in), will produce a continuous weir effect (see Photo 17), while stones or rocks fixed in a random position at angles down the fall will give a rippling rapid (Fig 43).

As already stressed, concrete and some types of natural stone can be harmful to plant and fish life. Limestone is definitely poisonous and should not be allowed in contact with the water. Any cement you use, whether as facing or for bedding in, must be treated as described in Chapter 7. If the surrounding mound of soil is to become a rockery and not just a grassy bank, I suggest completing the rockery work while you are making the watercourse. If you work the two together it will be easier to decide which stones to put in the water and which in the soil.

Many natural watercourses are in the form of a continuous fall. These can be copied quite easily in the water-garden layout, but the appearance can be unsightly when the pump is not working as you will get the effect of a dried-up stream. So, remember to design with small rock pools to break the fall and retain water.

There is yet another way to build your watercourse – the oldest of them all. Concrete has been used for many years, and I have no doubt that many people who have not closely studied the pleasing effects one can get with preformed or sheet liners will regard concrete as offering the most natural appearance. How-

Fig 36 The watercourse and steps are shaped in the bank of the soil

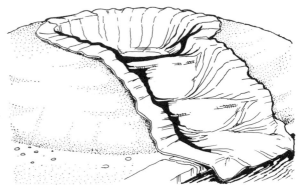

Fig 37 The liner is laid into the excavation and overlapped into the pool; where waterfall units are used they are placed in position and overlapped into the pool

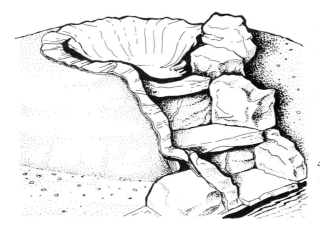

Fig 38 The stones are laid to form the falls and sides of the watercourse where necessary; the paving can be laid around the pool at this stage

Fig 39 The cement should be treated and the waterfall is ready for operation

ever, unless rock stone is cleverly incorporated, the appearance can be very stark. Although I have made a concrete pool, frankly I would not like to tackle a watercourse using this material. True, because there is less weight of water than in the pool, you will not need to make such elaborate preparations, but you will still have to lay a good firm base to take the cement.

The mixture is exactly the same as for a pool: 1 part cement, 2 of sand and 3 or 4 of aggregate, and this must be rendered and treated. Whether you smooth it off as you

should have done with the pool does not matter quite so much; over the many years it will remain usable the water will wear some of it away! But you will face the problem of the soil settling, and cracks are almost certain to develop at any time over the first few years, with consequent loss of water. In any case, because its lime content would enter the water and be carried down to the pool, with the already noted risks to fish and plants, you will have to treat the entire facing or seal it with a chlorinated rubber paint. However, if you do paint the surface, use a neutral stone-colour

86

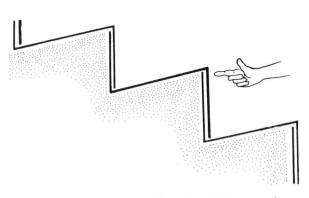

Fig 40 When more than one liner is used they must be overlapped on the fall

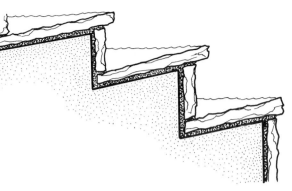

Fig 41 The channels are sloped to retain water when the pump is not in operation

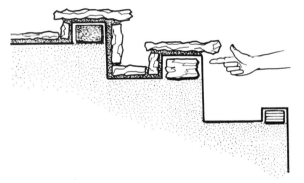

Fig 42 At the fall the liner can be raised using a stone underneath

Fig 43 Random stones placed in the waterfall provide a rapids effect

paint and not the bright blue which is more suitable for swimming pools.

It is not enough merely to lay a channel for the water to rush down. Rocks must be bedded in, and it is almost impossible to guarantee a completely watertight seal between rocks and the concrete. That is why, even when waterfalls are constructed in concrete, it is advisable to underline with plastic or butyl.

I have mentioned the wisdom of building the rockery at the same time as the waterfall. The point to watch here is soil washing down into the water. Wherever the rocks hold back the soil and there is this risk, the stones should be laid close together on a bed of mortar and the gaps between the rocks cemented to retain the soil. Use the cement at the back so as not to destroy the features of the rock face. Once the rockery is well established there will be no major problems. The plant roots will hold the soil quite effectively except in the most extreme conditions. All you really have to do is ensure that in these early stages you use the sand-cement holding mix so that the soil is not washed away from the vulnerable young roots, which would literally be left high and dry.

FLOW RATE

I have deliberately left until last an important technical point about watercourses. It concerns what is called the 'flow rate' – the volume of water passing through the system. If it comes through too fast it will disturb the balance of the pool; if it is too slow it will appear insignificant (see also Chapter 8).

It is all too easy for experts to talk about a flow of 1,365 lph (300gph), but what does this look like? Is it a trickle or a torrent? Your hosepipe fixed to a convenient running tap will give you a good indication of flow rates. To measure the hosepipe output, simply make a mark in a bucket at the 9 litre (2gal) level. Then check how long it takes the water to reach this level, and read off the rate against the time as shown in the accompanying table. Thus, if it takes 80sec the output is 405 lph (90gph).

Secs	lph	(gph)
20	1,620	(360)
30	1,080	(240)
40	810	(180)
50	648	(144)
60	540	(120)
70	462	(102)
80	405	(90)

With the output of the hose thus determined, turn it on down the waterfall to judge the effect. You may find that the output you want is two, three, or even ten times greater than the hose has given you, but this is much easier to assess once you have the evidence of a known output.

Pump capacity and tube bore size should really be considered together. My inclination is to use a slightly larger bore than the one you think you need. The additional cost is minimal and you can benefit from an increase in water output. The bore tubings adequate for various flow rates are as follows:

Bore		Max Flow Rate	
mm	(in)	lph	(gph)
13	(½)	546	(120)
19	(¾)	1,590	(350)
25	(1)	4,545	(1,000)
32	(1¼)	6,820	(1,500)
38	(1½)	13,638	(3,000)

These figures are based on average lengths of tubing, say up to 6m (20ft). On longer lengths, friction loss can be so great that you will have to use a bigger bore or a larger and more expensive pump.

10 Fountains and Water Features

JETS AND ORNAMENTS FOR THE POOL

Years ago fountains were used for purely functional purposes. In towns and cities water was piped to them for use by the population for drinking and washing. The Romans even had a fountain festival, when these water sources were decorated for the day. Communal drinking-bubble fountains are still common in all major cities, although it is unlikely that there are many of the older drinking fountains, with a cup chained to them, in existence.

In Britain, during Victorian times, there were many extremely ornate fountains. There were few pumps as we know them, so mostly they were fed by water piped from streams or reservoirs several feet above; the gravity force acting on a small hole was enough to form a jet. The fountain was operated by an inlet valve that could be turned on and off as required. The higher the level of supply, the better the performance. Fountains still have a magnetic attraction and form focal points like the Trevi fountain in Rome, Manneken Pis in Brussels and the Trafalgar Square fountains in London so enjoyed by New Year's Eve revellers. The magnificent Versailles fountains were built by King Louis XIV of France, whilst the fountain in Lake Geneva reaches a height of over 120m (400ft).

On a more humble note fountains can be brought into every garden. Enjoy the splashing sound, catch the myriad specks of light reflected from the sun, feel the refreshing coolness on a hot day or evening, and for that matter enjoy the flight of the birds as they come to bathe in the spray – you have a feature that will never bore. Below-the-water assets are that this movement maintains the oxygen in the water and, provided the surrounding pool is planted properly, you will never have a stagnation problem.

A fountain jet can create considerable turbulence. Many are set up for the express purpose of bringing about this effect, but you have to be careful where you site them in a water garden, for water-lilies in particular do not like turbulence and their blooms could easily be swamped. The fountain spray must therefore be kept well away from lilies, or in very small pools the fountain height must be restricted so that it does not fall on them. The oxygenating plants are not affected because they are largely below water level and so are cushioned.

Surprising as it may seem, the use of a fountain in a water garden is the subject of considerable controversy. Purists insist that a fountain has no place in an informal or natural pool, and should be used only in a purely formal layout. This book, however, sets out to enumerate ways in which we can increase the enjoyment we get from our gardens. Purity and enjoyment may sometimes be incompatible bedfellows, but if a fountain in your garden gives you pleasure, wherever it may be sited, then go ahead and never mind the purists. Whatever the size or nature of your pool, a little spray of water breaking surface from somewhere within it is an attraction to the eye, and at least a source of interest.

There are various types of fountain. You can have a jet mounted at water level to provide a spray of predetermined pattern rising

Photo 18 Formal sunken pool with ornamental fountain feature

from the water surface. This is the most popular type of fountain feature for the water garden. In small pools it is usually mounted directly on top of a submersible pump, which is raised sufficiently to enable the jet to emerge just above the water level. As already explained, in some circumstances you can also run a waterfall from this unit.

Alternatively, the necessary tee-piece and tubing could operate a second fountain or waterside ornament. Larger installations are normally operated remotely by a larger submersible pump, or by a surface pump housed outside the pool with tubing to carry the water to the fountain.

Choice of jet is important with any fountain.

90

Photo 19 A bell fountain on an ornament in the middle of the pool

If the spray is too fine it could be blown well beyond the confines of the pool on a windy day (an inevitable risk with a small pool) and would involve reducing the height of the jet. You can overcome wind drift to some extent by either placing your fountain in a well-sheltered spot or by having a side-spouting feature. A further point to bear in mind is that a fine spray is not seen so easily from a distance, and there is not much point in installing a fountain if you cannot see it working. The larger the jets of water the more visible it will be, and the less chance of wind drift.

There are various types of spray-head, offering a wide choice of height, width and spray pattern. Most have a fixed spray pattern, but there have been tremendous advances lately in research and manufacture. A recent introduction has six interchangeable spray-heads to enable you to select the most suitable, or to change the spray pattern at will. There are swivel fountain jets, single-plume fountains and even revolving fountains which operate a spinning spray pattern. Some are designed to emerge from ornamental features such as shells or artificial water-lilies. Another worthy of mention operates spray patterns which change automatically, though it needs only a small pump to operate. The secret is a simple engineering device – as water enters the housing it rotates a 'waterwheel' which drives various cams operating individual jets giving a number of different spray patterns.

All these fountains are similar: they depend on water being forced through a number of small holes in the fountain jet. On passing through the holes, the water forms a predetermined pattern, the height of which depends on the volume passing through. However, there are a number of other types of fountain spray which are quite different.

Simple geyser jets are very attractive; they are usually operated at a low height so have the advantage that they do not disturb a wide area. They simply discharge a white frothy jet of water into the air by means of a special fitting that draws in air which mixes with the water. Bell-jets form an attractive shimmering umbrella of water in the shape of a bell, and likewise cause very little disturbance. These can be situated at water level, or mounted on top of a fountain ornament (see Photo 19). Alternatively you can have a flat millstone, with a gentle flow emerging from its centre and forming a rippling film of water over the stone before returning to the pool. Although not strictly a fountain, this can make an attractive feature in the pool. Ring-jets can also be incorporated into the water garden. These have adjustable jets fitted onto rings of various diameters. They usually spray water upwards onto various ornamental figures.

Next we come to fountain or pool-side ornaments. A wide range is available from specialist suppliers in various shapes resembling humans, animals, fish or creatures of mythology, all spouting water. Some are beautiful, some frankly grotesque. The principle is always the same: the water is pumped to a figure from where it issues forth in either a simple stream to fall back to base, or in a series of patterns (see Photo 18).

Irrespective of design, most work on the same idea of a tube mounted inside the figure, with a threaded connector at the top on to which the jet is screwed. Some, mainly those designed to operate at the side of the pool, merely spout water back into it. Nevertheless, with some it is possible to fix a swivel or angle-jet, and this will produce a spray.

Most of the fountain ornaments generally available are made of treated concrete (or 're-constructed stone' as they are sometimes described); but specialist suppliers can offer a further selection made of lead, bronze, copper, clay, earthenware, plastic, pottery or even a form of marble.

Lighting offers further forms of excitement. This is dealt with at greater length in Chapter 18, but is mentioned here because illumination from below the fountain gives a spectacular display at night. You can buy complete kits which include pump, fountain and underwater lamp in different colours including red, green, amber or blue. Even more spectacular, you can have a colour-changing disc which changes the colour automatically.

Finally, and the most advanced idea at the time of writing, is the 'musical fountain', where a series of illuminated jets change colour and height to the rhythm of a musical background. The rise and fall of the jets is controlled by electrical impulses actuated by the

Page 93 (above) Water-lily 'Firecrest'; *(below)* Water-lily 'Attraction'

music. It is a very ingenious device; the biggest I have seen so far is a tourist attraction so complicated it is run by a computer!

Once you have listed all your requirements you should find an item in a specialist catalogue that appears to answer your needs; the supplier will also be able to help you with any obscure point. I can confirm that these specialists do offer a remarkably good service. Not least of the benefits is that many of them provide ready-prepared kits for assembling fountains (or fountain ornaments) and waterfalls. They will also design and make up any kits to suit individual requirements.

Naturally, you can buy any pump you want individually, and get the accessories you need separately, but it is much more convenient (and probably cheaper) to buy a kit that comes complete with all the basic tubing, cable and fittings, together with assembly instructions. Assembly of these units is so simple that before you know where you are you have your fountain or waterfall, or both, ready to switch on. You are about to realise the enjoyment that movement of water in your garden can bring.

Yet there are still further horizons ahead. Your pool is living, but there is no life in it as yet. How plants and fish can enhance your enjoyment is explained in the chapters that follow.

Photo 20 A self-contained patio feature fountain

WITHOUT A POOL

Automatically we think of a fountain as a jet, or several jets of water, thrown in the air and descending as a spray in various sizes of droplets and casting various predetermined patterns while falling back into the pool. This is not necessarily so. You can have a fountain feature without a pool, sited in the garden, on a patio, or indoors – in fact anywhere you require, provided it is within reach of a power supply. Nor are fish or plants essentials; without them you can easily keep the water clear by treating periodically with an algicide. These are generally referred to as fountain features or patio fountains and are usually self-contained units which only require setting on level ground, filling with water and connecting to the nearest electrical supply. The smallest types are the indoor table-top fountains which operate from a small bowl, sometimes only 30cm (12in) diameter, and also act as humidifiers.

There are many specially designed patio fountains suitable for use either indoors or outdoors. Some consist of a single bowl with a simple fountain in the centre; others have a figure from which a fountain emerges, or they

Page 94 (above) Water-lily 'Marliacea Carnea'; *(below)* Water-lily *odorata sulphurea*

simply pour water back into the bowl. Then there are two- and three-tiered fountains which have bowls of varying diameter with water cascading down. Finally, some bowls have ring-jets fitted which spray water up to a second bowl or figure.

Other purpose-made kits are available for making a water feature with a choice of fountain, bell-jet, geyser or millstone effect; and these are supplied with a small glass-fibre tank. Obviously this small diameter will not catch the droplets of water, so also supplied is a square piece of plastic liner which is large enough to catch the water and return it to the tank. Also supplied with this kit is the pump, plastic lid to fit the tank and the chosen fountain (Fig 44).

These units can be installed at ground level, although it does mean making a small excavation to receive the tank. The liner is then laid on the ground but sloping slightly towards the tank. Alternatively, they can be raised by placing the tank at ground level and building walls 1·8m (6ft) square or round. The cavity between the tank and walls is filled with sand, and the plastic liner laid on this. Both types are usually finished by placing cobble stones over the area to hide the 'works'. They are most attractive when completed and make ideal features for patios, bringing water into play without the need for a pool.

Alternatively, you can design and make your water feature. Any bowl or tank will suffice provided it is deep enough to cover the pump and large enough to catch the water.

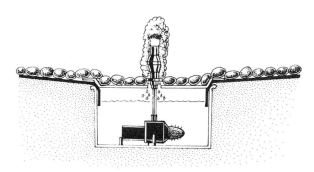

Fig 44 A cobbled fountain feature is ideal for a patio

Fountains or figures can be placed in the centre and connected to a pump. If the basin is ornamental the whole thing can be on display, otherwise the basin will have to be of sunken type.

Cobble-effect water features are easily installed and need only a small reservoir of water; they can be constructed at or above ground level as required. The reservoir can be made with a pool liner as previously described, but will need to be a minimum of 1·2m (4ft) either round or square. A chamber is built inside the reservoir using bricks, but with gaps so that water can enter freely. The pump is installed in the chamber and a mesh or lid placed on top. The surrounding area can be made up with old bricks (mind the sharp edges on the liner) and the top capped off with a layer of cobble stones or rocks. Usually these features have a geyser-type fountain or millstone, but they can also have the bell or a conventional fountain.

11 Filters for garden and Koi Pools

BASIC PRINCIPLES

In a well-stocked garden pool, the plants are easily capable of maintaining clear water and a healthy environment for fish. In new ponds this may take a period of time, during which the water often becomes 'green' due to algae formation. When the oxygenators and the small animals that feed on algae become established the water should clear. Very occasionally a pond that is correctly planted does suffer from water that remains 'green', due to a number of factors, often interrelated. If the water is particularly rich in minerals, which may have leached from the soil in planting baskets or may simply be in the water supply, algae will flourish. Alternatively there may not be enough shade on the pond, so too much light is the cause. With really stubborn cases of green water a filter will solve the problem.

A filter system is essential where there are no plants, or where there is an unnaturally high fish stocking density – usually in pools that have been constructed specifically for Koi carp. Large Koi of over 30cm (12in) will overturn planting crates, uproot aquatic plants and eat the oxygenators. In these conditions, only a filter system will clear and purify the water, which the fish are continually polluting with their waste matter. Such pools are specialist installations and not strictly water gardens, but because many pool owners do extend their interests to Koi, a brief review of how they work is included (page 66).

There are two types of filter (out of the many used in industry) of interest to the water gardener – mechanical and biological. Most are sited outside the pool. When choosing or constructing one it is essential to consider your requirements and select the correct type. In garden ponds where algae are the problem, continuously running mechanical filters (resulting in a certain amount of biological activity) are probably to be preferred. These can also be used in Koi ponds in addition to a biological filter. As well as the right type of filter, the correct size must be used. A small gravel filter may keep a small pond crystal clear, but would have little effect on a much larger volume of water. Often a filter that is considered useless is simply not big enough to cope with the demands placed on it.

The small gauzes on the intake of pumps are often referred to as filters. Don't be misled by this description. In reality they are simply strainers and are useful only to prevent dirt or grit blocking the pump impeller.

Mechanical Filters

The mechanical filter acts as a trap for small particles of matter, and works like a sieve, catching objects larger than its pore size. As more debris is trapped so the available pore size decreases, allowing finer particles to be caught. Eventually the system is self-defeating as the pores become clogged. Obviously the size of the pore and the amount and size of the debris has to be considered. Fine pores would soon block up if there were a large quantity of suspended matter. Consequently mechanical filters are often used in series, with larger filter pores, to remove most of the debris, then smaller pores to eliminate the finer particles.

Mechanical filters remove solid debris but have little effect in purifying the water.

Biological Filters

In biological filters, aerated water passes over an object, for example plastic or stone, which acts as a base on which nitrifying bacteria colonies form. These break down fish body-wastes and are accompanied by many other microscopic creatures some of which digest algae, and others small organic matter. This forms the basis of all biological filter systems.

In their simplest form they consist of a container, full of a substrate (filter media) through which water can flow. Pore spaces between the substrate should be fairly large so that the flow of water is not impaired and a continuous flow is available to the bacteria. In effect, the natural purifying agents of a pond have thus been increased and concentrated in one area.

Fish produce (as a by-product of body metabolism) large amounts of ammonia that passes out of the gills and into the water. In large volumes of water this instantly dilutes to an insignificant proportion, but in a small pool would soon accumulate to a level capable of poisoning the fish. The nitrifying bacteria that colonise biological filters convert ammonia to a harmless substance. In addition the filter breaks down excreta into ammonia, which again is converted by the bacteria.

GARDEN-POOL FILTERS

In garden ponds, any pollution is normally due to either algae or debris on the pool base which is 'stirred up' by the fish. This may be in the form of decaying plants, or soil that has washed out of their baskets. As the stocking density is low there is very little dissolved pollution due to fish waste. Ammonia excreted from the gills becomes diluted immediately by the water to an extremely low concentration, which is easily converted by the resident pond bacteria to a harmless plant fertiliser. Here the usual choice is the mechanical filter as the pollution is of a 'solid' nature.

A common mechanical filter is the pressurised sand-filter normally used for swimming pools, where the pores are provided by the space between the grains of sand. The latter have to be used with a high-pressure pump, as the spaces between the sand grains are extremely small. The filter body is totally enclosed, making a pressurised system when the pump is operated. If larger pores are desired, sand is removed from the filter and replaced with a larger gravel.

In operation, water is pumped under pressure through the sand, before being returned to the pool. As the sand will eventually clog up, a facility for backwashing has to be incorporated. Normally this is carried out by a special valve that reverses the water-flow through the sand (so clearing it of debris) and simultaneously diverts it to a different outlet leading to a drain.

Another type of mechnical filter uses thick layers of open-cell sponge. These sponges are a recent introduction to garden-pond filtration systems and in most cases have proved effective in removing algae. They are placed in a non-pressurised container, and water passes through them by gravity. With continuous operation, bacterial colonies can grow on the filtering material. Sponge filters are ideal for the garden pool, where they are often used to bolster the nitrifying bacteria present (Fig 45).

Fig 45 With a sponge filter, water is pumped through a spray bar, filters through to the outlet tube and flows back to the pool

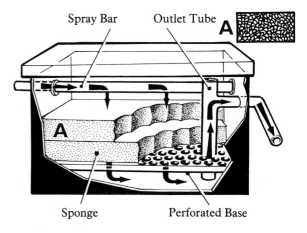

Spray Bar Outlet Tube A

A

Sponge   Perforated Base

Filters discussed so far have been external types, sited outside the pool and connected to it by pipework. Small pools under 3·7m² (40sq ft) which are difficult to keep free from algae often benefit by the use of an internal filter, consisting of a perforated tray supporting gravel attached to the intake of the pump. Again, although primarily a mechanical filter, a secondary biological action can be started if it is operated continuously. The only advantage these have over external filters is that they remain hidden in the pond.

KOI-POOL FILTERS

Any pool that contains fish but has no plants is an unnatural environment and poses different water-pollution problems. In addition these ponds are often stocked far beyond normal densities, as without the plant life to fill in and complete the effect the pond would appear almost empty. The water pollution in this case is caused almost entirely by the fish. Fish pollute water in two ways. Undigested food passes through and is removed from the body as excrement. Often the worst of this can be removed using a bottom drain as discussed in Koi-pond construction (page 66) or, in extreme cases, a settling tank as described overleaf. Potentially more dangerous is ammonia, which fish excrete through the gills. Basically, it is formed from the breakdown of proteins the body no longer needs, and is extremely toxic. Unless it is removed the fish will poison themselves.

Mechanical filters are not effective in this case: the ammonia is actually dissolved in the water, and cannot be sieved out. The only practical solution is to use a biological filter, the main function of which is to convert ammonia to nitrate, which is relatively harmless.

There are different types of biological filter; one is similar to an undergravel filter in an aquarium and is constructed within the pool. These internal filters are not suitable for Koi pools. Often they form a fibrous, wool-like coating on the surface impeding the water, which instead of flowing through the substrate in a uniform manner finds just a few channels, often down the inside of the filter case. In addition, Koi are capable of removing the filter media and distributing it around the pool. External pond filters, housed in a separate chamber, are understandably more efficient.

The size and type of the filter media is important in biological filters. If it is too small, it will clog up like a mechanical filter; though it does present a larger surface area for colonisation by bacteria. The best compromise is to use one of specially designed plastic media, or angular gravel, averaging 2·5cm (1in) in length.

The size of the filter governs its effectiveness. It should be at least one-eighth the volume of the pool, with the substrate about 1m (3ft) deep. Allow 4,545 litres per hour (1,000gph) water-flow per ·7m³ (cubic yard) of filter to provide adequate aeration. Although the volume of the filter has been related to that of the pond, of equal importance is the weight of fish it can support. A good rule of thumb here is that ·7m³ (1cu yd) of media will support 23kg (50lb) of fish, if there is adequate aeration. This can be achieved by spraying the water onto the filter surface, using a spray-bar or jet nozzles. Insufficient aeration results in areas of the filter being unable to sustain the nitrifying bacteria. In their place anaerobic bacteria, capable of living without oxygen, would form. These break down nutrients in the water into chemicals harmful to fish.

In a new pond it would take approximately ten weeks for the bacteria colonies to establish, so the initial stocking of fish should be low. Unlike the situation when setting up a waterfall, the pump should be at the opposite end of the pool from the filter to ensure that all the water is filtered.

External filters are often made of fibre glass, or constructed of concrete blocks reinforced with metal rods down the centre. Depending upon the substrate to be used, the base of the

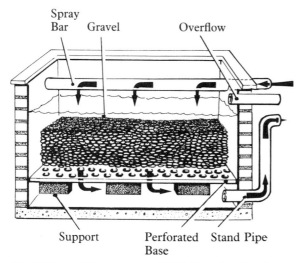

Fig 46 A specially constructed Koi filter showing the passage of water

filter will have to be strengthened accordingly – obviously, a filter using stone chippings will have to be stronger than one containing plastic media. If the filter casing has been constructed of concrete blocks it must be made watertight, using any of the methods suggested in pool construction, although a liner is easiest.

Using a tank connector, fit a stand-pipe into the liner as close to the base as possible. This controls the level of water in the container and should be adjusted so that approximately 8cm (3in) of water covers the top of the media. A 5cm (2in) diameter stand-pipe will cope with

about 4,545 litres per hour (1,000gph). A false base has then to be inserted above the connection of the stand-pipe to the filter. This can be made of thick plastic sheet perforated with 13mm (½in) holes 15cm (6in) apart, supported on bricks. In addition to the stand-pipe, an overflow above the stand-pipe level should be provided as an extra precaution (Fig 46).

In operation water is sprayed onto the filter surface, percolates through the substrate, flows into the stand-pipe and returns to the pool either through tubing or a waterfall.

SETTLING TANKS

Settling tanks may be used to remove some of the heavy debris before it reaches the filter, thus helping to prevent blockage of mechanical filters, or overloading of biological ones. They are simply a container through which water flows. The slower the flow the more debris settles out but, as the filter often requires a fast flow-rate, a compromise will have to be made. As a guide, a pool of 4,545 litres (1,000gal) should have a settling tank of about ·4m³ (½cu yd) with a flow of 1,365–2,275 litres per hour (300–500gph) passing through.

These tanks are necessary only in extremely heavily stocked ponds, or where large amounts of debris are either produced or fall into the water.

12 Principles of Planting: Pests and Diseases

ESSENTIALS TO REMEMBER

When equipping the pool it may not be possible to realise all your ambitions. You should not, for instance, have a large fountain and waterfall unless the pool has a large surface area; for while plants will tolerate a gentle ripple from a waterfall or stream, they cannot endure the ceaseless drumming of water from a fountain on their leaves or petals. You can overcome this problem by the old mixture of moderation and compromise, and if you can refrain from going over the top in this respect you will achieve a perfectly acceptable result. Lilies and other surface plants will prosper if set beyond the range of the falling fountain drops – rain has to be accepted by them!

This aspect apart, furnishing a water garden does impose certain disciplines. The first is that you must not be in too much hurry; fill the pool with water a few days before planting. There are two main reasons for this. One is to get the water to the relevant ambient temperature; the other is to let it 'mature', giving time for any harmful chemicals and other impurities to disperse. If you have a concrete pool you will need to treat it to neutralise the lime content, as explained earlier. Another rule is that, although with orthodox garden plants it is customary to plant them out while they are more or less dormant, water plants generally are best planted in their early growing season. Luckily for the owner, this usually coincides with the best working conditions of spring and early summer. Nor is this all. You cannot start by planting exactly what you want to the exclusion of everything else. Your main desire may be to produce a glorious carpeting of glamorous and exotic water-lilies, but other plants are equally important.

The well-equipped water garden is fitted out very comprehensively (Fig 47). You will have oxygenators, marginal plants, deep-marginal plants, floating plants and, of course, water-lilies. You may also have a few snails. These may play little part in delighting your senses (or your visitors'), but don't reject them out of hand. In normal conventional gardens we may reach for the slug pellets as soon as we see an infestation, but certain varieties of aquatic snails have a useful purpose in the water garden and do earn their keep. In the USA one snail, *Viviparus maniatus* is highly recommended whilst in Britain the Ramshorn (*Planorbus corneus*) is favoured.

All planting in any garden should be done with a purpose, and this is even more critical in a water garden. Firstly, you must provide a suitable home for the fish – assuming, of course, that you have not decided to deprive yourself of the pleasures of their company. This involves planting oxygenators to use up their waste products and to provide them with oxygen. The fish will also need shade, which is provided by the lilies and floating plants.

Then you will need plants to combat algae. It is no use having a fine collection of fish if the water is too green to see them. In a mature pool 60 to 70 per cent of the surface should be covered with the foliage of water-lilies, floating and deep-marginal plants, this will reduce the amount of sunlight entering the water – one of the main causes of algae; the other main cause, an abundance of mineral salts, will be countered by the oxygenating plants.

101

Fig 47 A well-established water garden fitted out comprehensively with oxygenators, marginal plants, deep-marginal plants, floating plants and water-lilies

Most specialist suppliers offer a complete collection of plants for a given surface area. Typically, for a pool of $3 \cdot 7 m^2$ (40sq ft), a pack will include 2 water-lilies, 18 oxygenating plants, 6 marginal and 4 floating plants. This makes selection much easier, and as the new water gardener gains knowledge and experience he can add or exchange varieties without disturbing the balance of his pool collection.

Some people make a pool purely to keep fish, and plants are the last thing they want. Inevitably there will be algae and fish waste matter to combat and a very efficient filtration system will have to be installed to keep the water pure and fresh. The vast majority of pool owners, however, want the best of both worlds – exotic fish and beautiful flowering plants. To them a water garden means precisely that – a garden in water.

To get the best effects, it is necessary to understand the function or purpose of each category of plant used. They can, as already indicated, generally be divided into five groups:

Photo 21 Marginal plants are better in groups than placed singly around the pool

    water-lilies
    oxygenating plants
    floating plants
    marginal plants
    deep-marginals

All, collectively, are useful to create a natural biological balance within the pool.

There is a further classification – bog and moisture-loving plants – which inhabit the no-man's-land between the pool and the orthodox garden. They need a damp situation, but not so wet as the marginals nor so dry as most conventional herbaceous plants (see Chapter 14).

WATER-LILIES (Nymphaeas)

Here is the crowning glory of the water garden – the embodiment of awe and majesty; for who has not gasped in admiration at a display of water-lilies in flower? And there are so many of them, in so many shapes, sizes and beautiful colours. Even the leaves are attractive; some varieties being apple green, some a greeny purple. Copper and yellow-flowered hardy varieties all have speckled leaves – an attractive brown or purple on a green background.

Blooms of the *Nymphaea*, to give them their generic name, were offered by the ancient Egyptians to their gods, so drawings and writings featuring the water-lily can be traced back thousands of years. They are native to most parts of the world, many countries claiming at least one native species; the British *N. alba* can be seen growing on the edges of lakes and natural ponds almost anywhere in the country.

Water-lilies are divided into two groups – hardy and tropical. For obvious reasons, the tropicals are comparatively limited as regards the regions where they can be successfully grown outdoors, so there is a greater call for the hardy types. Most of the brightly coloured hardy varieties that heighten the scene in garden pools today owe their existence to a Frenchman, Bory Latour-Marliac, who in the last two decades of the nineteenth century produced a stream of brilliant hybrids. Many are still popular today, though modern hybridisers, notably in the USA, have brought us an even wider range, building on the foundations he laid.

Although water-lilies are undoubtedly the most spectacular of all water plants since no other bloom adorns a pool so colourfully and exercises such fascination for pool owner and visitor, they are not just decorative. The leaves fulfil a very useful function in providing shade that deprives algae of sunlight, at the same time enabling the fish to play hide-and-seek with us. Indeed, when it comes to the ecology of the pool, the leaves are of even greater value than the blooms.

Hardy lilies have one of two distinct root systems. The tuberosa types have creeping rootstocks and are planted almost horizontally, but with the crown slightly above soil level. Others have a more vertical rootstock and have to be planted upright, again with the crown above the soil level.

In an established pool 60 to 70 per cent of the surface area should be covered with foliage, as suggested previously. In most pools, marginal and floating plants will cover some of the surface, so as a rule-of-thumb reckoning you should plan to cover between 40 and 50 per cent with lily leaves. Sizes of these vary enormously. The pygmaea types have leaves only some 5cm (2in) in diameter, but some of the more vigorous varieties have leaves up to 38 to 45cm (15 to 18in) across, so care must be taken over selection. The pygmaeas will grow in 8 to 23cm (3 to 9in) of water, but should be given winter protection at the shallower depths as they are vulnerable in a severe winter. Others will grow happily at anything from 15cm (6in) to ·9m or 1·2m (3 or 4ft).

It is difficult to be specific on the number of water-lilies needed for a given pool surface because plants vary in size and vigour. Remembering that one single water-lily can occupy up to 2·3m² (25sq ft) of surface water, for a pool of say 3·7m² (40sq ft) you would expect to accommodate one large variety or two mediums or three or four small/miniature ones. Vigour and surface spread are indicated in the section on water-lilies in Chapter 13.

As with most aquatics, lilies should be introduced to the pool gradually. Stand them

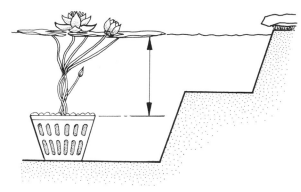

Fig 48 The planting depth for water-lilies is measured from the top of the crate to the water level

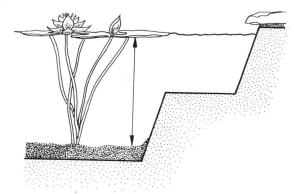

Fig 49 Where water-lilies are planted in soil at the bottom of the pool, the planting depth is measured from water level to soil

on blocks or bricks at first and gradually lower them to the bottom. In the early stages the top of the crate should not be more than about 15 to 23cm (6 to 9in) below the water surface (Fig 48). When planting in pockets this is impossible, so the lily should be planted in the bottom and the pool filled with water over a number of weeks. The planting depth is the amount of water over the soil (Fig 49).

This precaution is important. Planting too deeply at the start is asking for trouble; failure to establish being the most common penalty. Lilies normally take some time to feel comfortable and at home; for instance, they are unlikely to flower in their first season unless planted very early. There are other causes of initial alarm. At first the flowers are almost certain to be smaller and paler than seen in a catalogue or at a specialist supplier's pool. This is natural, and due to the upheaval. When the plant has established, the flowers will gain their true colour. Similarly, when a lily is lifted it may have leaves some 45cm (18in) across, but after replanting new leaves may be only a quarter of that size. They will gradually return to their full size as the lily establishes again. Don't forget, also, that some varieties have small leaves anyway; not all are 45cm (18in) giants. Even more alarming, perhaps, is the sight of a bud that refuses

to open. This, too, is purely first-season reaction; all will come well eventually.

A further cause of panic is the sight of the leaves turning brown and dying. But water-lily leaves are constantly renewed throughout the season. They come to the surface and unfurl on the water; after three or four weeks they turn yellow, sink below the surface, and gradually decay, to feed the new growth. If you regard yellowing leaves as unsightly you can snip them off, and in fact this is recommended in August and September.

Failure to flower after becoming established is another fairly common complaint. Incorrect planting depth is one reason. Or there could be insufficient sunlight, which could indicate an original error in siting the pool. Alternatively, the planting medium is poor. An obvious remedy is to replant in good soil, or you can treat with a special lily fertiliser. One other possible cause remains, and it brings us back to a point mentioned at the beginning of the chapter – the incompatibility of fountains and water-lilies in too-close proximity. Site your *Nymphaeas* too close to moving water, whether from a fountain, a waterfall, or just a current, and you will inhibit their progress. The remedy is obvious.

Blooms are produced in constant succession from mid-June until late September according

104

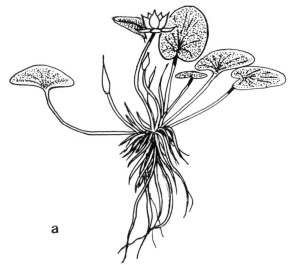

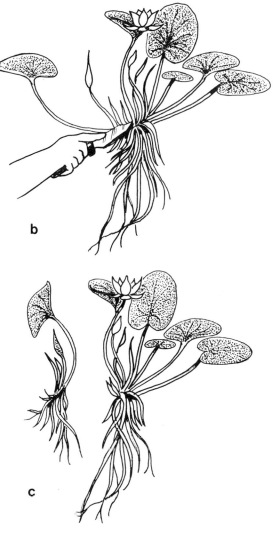

Fig 50 An established lily requires dividing:
a The plant is removed from its container and washed off.
b When there is more than one crown, select a strong growing young side shoot as this will establish more quickly than an older crown.
c With a sharp knife cut the smaller crown off the old rhizome and replant as described.

to location and weather. Each bloom lasts for three to five days, after which it sinks under the water and rots away. Water-lilies die back in October when the water temperature drops or the frosts come. With most, growth starts again in March as soon as the water temperature increases, but miniature varieties do not show again until May.

Water-lilies need very little attention. Once every three to six years, depending upon variety, they will require lifting and replanting, and they give unmistakable warning when that time arrives. Instead of lying flat on the water surface the leaves are thrust high above it, thus greatly reducing the display of flowers. In addition, those thrusting leaves are not nearly so attractive as those sitting serenely on the water! When replanting, lift the lily from the pool (April or May is the best time) and wash off all the soil. You will find a main crown probably on an old thick rhizome. Ignore this one, for it is not the best bet for replanting. Choose instead a smaller but

strong and healthy sideshoot, and cut this away from the main rhizome. It will have much more vigour, and will transplant well with a much better chance of success (Fig 50). The hardy varieties, as you would expect, remain in the pool throughout the year and do not require any special frost protection.

Tropicals, though having much the same characteristics, are generally even more attractive than the hardy varieties. They have large leaves (some crinkled) with bigger and yet more colourful flowers. Many have a scent; some bloom by day and others at night. Naturally they are somewhat more tender, so in

105

Photo 22 A large pool with bold planting of water-lilies

temperate climates they must not be planted until the water has really warmed up – usually up to a month after the hardy types – and must be protected against frost. Their leaves are comparatively thin, so because there is a great risk of drying out they must be kept thoroughly damp at all times while planting. In the USA some suppliers recommend that the container should be prepared and installed first, so that the crown and leaves go straight into the water when planted.

Obviously, these lilies do well in tropical areas including parts of the USA, Australia and southern Europe; but in temperate zones they have to rely on a hot summer if they are to thrive. Here, the only alternative to keeping them in a heated area indoors is to lift them from an outdoor pool in good time before the frosts. Cut away and discard the old thick tubers and store the new young tubers in dry,

clean sand through the winter in frost-free conditions, replanting around late May to June depending on the weather. Few gardeners will want the inconvenience that this entails.

Some varieties lend themselves to 'specimen treatment' – a single crown planted in a tub half full of soil and under 20cm (8in) of water. A wine tub or half a beer barrel makes an excellent container. Move them indoors in autumn.

Having said this, for practical purposes it is better, if you live in a temperate zone, to confine your selection to the hardy types. This is no great hardship, for there are plenty from which to choose. In fact, most specialists supply only the hardy varieties.

OXYGENATING PLANTS
For a garden pool to be a complete success so that both plants and fish flourish, one important thing is essential – clear and unpolluted water. The one way in which this can be maintained, other than by repeated draining and

106

refilling, is to plant a sufficient number of submerged oxygenating aquatics in conjunction with a balance of floating aquatics and water-lilies.

Although the lowliest and cheapest types of plant for the water garden, oxygenators are in many ways the most important. Like most plants, under the influence of sunlight they absorb carbon dioxide and provide oxygen; however, at night the process is reversed so this is not their chief attribute. One of their main purposes is to win the battle against algae and thereby help to keep the water clear. They live on the mineral salts in the water, as do algae, and because their appetite is greater they starve the latter. They also require sunlight, which is the other ingredient needed by algae if they are to thrive.

Another main function is in maintaining the balance between fish and their environment. When fish are introduced into a bare pool their waste products accumulate and produce a high, often fatal, level of toxic ammonia. (This is why goldfish won at a fair and kept in a goldfish bowl often soon die: they are gradually poisoned by their own waste matter.) The ammonia is broken down by bacteria in the water into nitrates, which although still fairly toxic will be readily absorbed by plants, particularly oxygenators, which convert them into plant proteins.

Nor does this end the usefulness of oxygenators. They provide a natural vegetable diet for the fish, and at spawning time it is likely the eggs will be deposited among the lush growth of these plants. Even when the fry hatch, the numbers that survive will depend on the oxygenators; their dense patches providing a perfect hiding place for the youngsters in thwarting their parents' cannibalistic habits.

Oxygenating plants are usually supplied in bunches of unrooted cuttings. Because they are a natural food for fish, there is some danger that the plants may all be eaten. Plant them at least two weeks before you introduce the fish,

so that the latter cannot destroy them – as they would given the chance – before the roots become established. The fish snatch at the oxygenators and, if the roots give, the plants rise to the surface and are chewed away. Established plants are constantly nibbled, but as a snack and not devoured as a feast, so the leaves are quickly replenished and no harm is done. If there are difficulties in introducing plants first, for instance if you are bringing new plants to a pool already well stocked with fish, grow the oxygenators in a separate tank or pool for two or three weeks to become established and then put them in the pool. They will grow faster than the fish can eat them, and once established it will be practically impossible for the fish to dislodge them.

If this plan is not feasible try growing Hornwort (*Ceratophyllum*), which for some reason fish do not seem partial to. It is an extraordinary little plant. Because it does not set roots you simply place it in the water and it will thrive. Fish love it for spawning.

Most oxygenators thrive at around 45 to 60cm (18 to 24in) depth which for practical purposes is the best depth for most garden pools, though they can be planted at anything from 23cm (9in) to 1·2m (4ft). For example, *Tillaea recurva* is not only adaptable to either a shallow or a deep pool, but for good measure can also actually grow above the water surface. This, like *Callitriche autumnalis*, is the equivalent of a water-garden evergreen, for its tiny bright-green leaves continue to flourish from autumn through to spring – a valuable asset. Planting is simple. With a finger, a hole is made in the soil in a planting crate and the weighted end of the bunch is planted and firmed. Then the crate is topped with gravel and placed on the bottom of the pool. The normal planting rate is one bunch for each 2m^2 (2sq ft) of water surface, though this rate can be reduced for larger pools.

A few oxygenators even have significant flowers. The Water Buttercup (*Ranunculus aquatilis*) produces masses of snow-white blooms in spring and summer. Another excellent flowering example is the Water Violet (*Hottonia palustris*), which has lilac/white flowers. These two are, however, reluctant to establish themselves, so be prepared for disappointments.

Many experts declare that the best of all oxygenating plants is *Lagarosiphon major*, with peculiar long narrow 'stems' of curled leaves reaching up through the water. It is certainly one of the most active of the oxygenators.

Remember that these oxygenators are, in effect, weeds, though unlike most of their herbaceous counterparts they do justify their existence. But they too, can become too enthusiastic and grow in the wrong place, so occasionally they need thinning out. Luckily, the system of planting them in crates helps to keep them within bounds, but after the first season you may find that even then some plants are getting too rampant. Excessive growth can be trimmed by simply cutting it back with a sharp knife. This will prevent the plant becoming straggly and it will grow bushy and compact.

A word of warning here. Oxygenators should not be left unattended for long periods and then slashed back to virtually nothing; this can allow algae to regain a foothold. Trim back little and often.

FLOATING PLANTS

This is an important group of plants for providing shade to help combat algae, particularly in the first year after initial planting of the pool during which the water-lily leaves will not be able to take on this function. When the pool is established the mature lily leaves will provide this service and the floating plants can be reduced.

Floating plants, too, can be divided into two groups – hardy and tropical. There are but few hardy species and this is why the list in Chapter 13 is supplemented with tropical varieties. In temperate zones the latter must not be put outdoors until all frosts have finished and this

is usually between mid May and early June, depending upon where you live. For over-wintering, all tropical plants should be removed from the pool by early September. They are very susceptible to early and late frost, and though there may be no apparent surface damage there could easily be a delayed reaction. A shallow bowl with a layer of soil and a few inches of water should provide a good home. Keep them at a minimum temperature of 10–13°C (50–55°F). Don't bother about giving them feed or fertiliser; this is their dormant season, so they do not need any form of stimulant. Keep them in a light position, possibly on a window ledge. Remember, however, to bring them into the room at night and not imprison them between curtain and window.

Two tropicals are particularly attractive and well worth growing, even if they are treated as annuals and discarded at the end of the season. Water Chestnut (*Trapa natans*) produces edible chestnuts in a good season, though the British climate rarely allows it to reach this stage. There is, however, the consolation of a show of tiny white flowers and attractive rosettes of olive-green leaves. The Water Hyacinth (*Eichhornia crassipes*) is another beauty well worth cultivating. Its main resemblance to the conventional hyacinth is that the flowers are borne on spikes, but it is one of the most attractive of all water plants.

Some of the hardy floating plants, particularly Lemnas and Azolla, can multiply and spread at a phenomenal rate in pools with a plentiful supply of mineral salts. For this reason they are not recommended for large pools and lakes, for they have to be removed and this can be difficult with a large surface. In smaller pools this is not a problem; you merely turn the hose on them and wash them to the side, where they can easily be netted off. Lemnas die off in winter, and over-wintering spores lie dormant on the bottom of the pool, emerging again in the spring.

Stratiotes is an excellent hardy floater. It

produces new plants from runners sent out from the parent plant, and these break off as the young plant matures. When they become too plentiful, the older plants can be removed and disposed of, leaving the youthful offspring to produce further new plants. Hydrocharis dies back to small buds in autumn; these drop to the bottom of the pool and re-emerge in May. Watch carefully if you empty and clean the pool in the 'off season', for these buds will be lying in the mud in a dormant state and could easily be thrown away.

Floating plants exist without soil. They take their nutrients directly from the water and, because they have no anchoring roots, are liable to turn up more or less anywhere on the surface. Like oxygenators, they feed on the mineral salts, thus keeping algae growth to a minimum.

MARGINAL PLANTS

These are grown more for their ornamental effect than as contributors to the ecological balance of the pool. However, they do provide a certain amount of surface shade, thus limiting algae, and they also offer some protection against the worst of the biting winds that can occur in exposed locations; water-lilies, which prefer quiet still water, can benefit from this.

Marginals are planted around the pool with their feet in the water and their foliage above the surface (see Photo 21). These are the plants for which you should have provided a ledge or shelf when building the pool (Fig 51). Many of them have beautiful flowers, whilst others are grown mainly for their foliage. Some knowledge is necessary in dealing with them for they thrive at different depths; some require planting at water level whilst others prefer to be 15cm (6in) or more under water. It is important to understand what is meant by 'planting depth'. In normal gardening it refers to the depth to which a plant is put in the soil. In water gardening 'planting depth' is the distance under water, and is measured from the top of the soil to the water level (Fig 52).

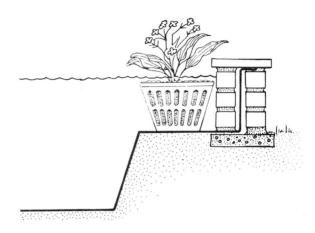

Fig 51 Provision should be made at the construction stage for marginal plants as shown in this half-raised pool

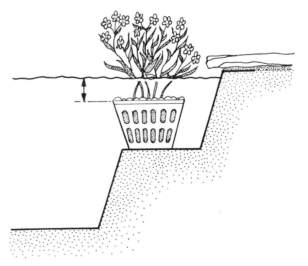

Fig 52 The planting depth for marginals is measured from the top of the crate to water level

109

Frequently, an acclimatising technique is employed as with water-lilies. In the early stages the crate is stood on tiles or bricks to give a shallower planting depth, and this block is later removed as the plant grows and establishes itself.

Some varieties are invasive but this should not be a problem if using planting crates. However, prudence suggests that each crate should contain only plants of the same variety, since a rapid and prolific grower could quickly engulf its partner.

Marginals form the greater part of the pool population and there are more of them from which to choose. They include many names familiar in orthodox herbaceous gardening – Calthas (Marsh Marigolds), Irises in a great range of colours and varieties, Ranunculus and waterside versions of Lobelia, Forget-me-not and Mint.

Marginals need occasional lifting, dividing and replanting, but otherwise they demand little attention. Most start into growth in March though some species, notably the Sagittarias, do not show until late May. They die back in October, but leave them until November and then cut back the dead foliage to within a few inches of the container. This procedure is not essential for the well-being of the plant, but is done for tidiness and to remove pests that are overwintering in the foliage. Some marginals have an upright habit, while others creep over the surface. Calla, Menyanthes, Myriophyllum (especially) and Veronica have this spreading habit, and when they have strayed too far should be trimmed back and replanted in their original position.

Among this group, Cotula is the only species regarded as a true annual. You can remove a few seed-heads in August and store them, then sow directly into their container in May, where they will flourish. Alternatively, you can sow them into a small pot indoors in April; after germinating they can be planted in the pool in late May.

DEEP MARGINALS

Only a few plants come into this category, but they include some of the most interesting in the whole water garden. Some have leaves that float on the water in a similar manner to the water-lily, and in smaller pools they are often used instead of it. Usually, however, both are grown together, and make an appealing contrast. Aponogeton gives colour before and after the normal flowering season of the water-lily.

As their name implies, deep marginals are usually planted in the bottom of the pool, but while some produce floating leaves and flowers others poke their leaves and flowers defiantly above the water.

PLANTING METHODS

For many years the only method recommended for planting a pool was to cover the base and the marginal ledge with a 15cm (6in) layer of soil (Fig 53). Water-lilies, oxygenators, marginals and deep marginals were then planted directly into the soil and the pool was filled very slowly over two to three weeks to allow the plants to establish their leaves, which would gradually extend with the rising surface of water. Marginals had to be watered regularly until the water level rose to reach them.

There were, and are, two major drawbacks to this system. In the first place fish, particularly tench and Koi carp but also to a lesser extent goldfish and shubunkins, root around in the soil causing the water to remain constantly cloudy. This condition can largely be eliminated by introducing only surface-feeding fish such as orfe and rudd, which do not have a tendency to root in the mud.

The second problem is more serious, for it will worsen after a period of time. For the first year or so everything will be fine – the plants

Page 111 A delightful garden incorporating a rockery and waterfall

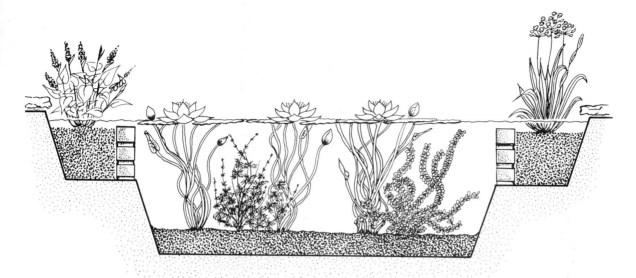

Fig 53 A traditional planting scheme in pools, with a layer of soil on the bottom

will grow vigorously and will soon establish. But this is where the problem arises, for many plants will grow too vigorously, and very soon the rampant growers will smother the more choice varieties and choke them out. Only the strong will survive. The situation can be controlled by a vigorous programme of weeding, but this is a time-consuming and thankless job and has the disadvantage that it will stir the mud at the bottom of the pool and so cloud the water.

In Pockets

A better way is to construct purpose-made planting pockets around the edge of the pool, so that marginal plants can be planted in these pockets. This is easier if provision has been made at the construction stage, because the marginal shelf will have been made 8 to 10cm (3 to 4in) wider than for planting crates. With this system, the planting shelf will be approximately 30cm (12in) wide, and a retaining wall must be built up on this shelf. The pocket is then filled with good soil and capped with gravel. Pockets do not have to be made all round the pool: they can be constructed as and where desired (Fig 54). The only problem with marginals planted this way is that inva-

Page 112 (above) Sagittaria japonica 'Flore Pleno'; *(below) Orontium aquaticum*

113

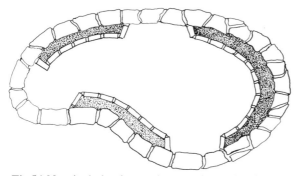

Fig 54 Marginal planting pockets can be made where required around the perimeter of the pool

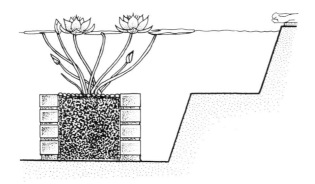

Fig 55 Water-lily planting pockets built in the pool

Fig 56 The newly planted pool showing the crates raised on blocks

sive or strong-growing varieties can quickly overgrow more choice but less vigorous varieties. Plants suitable for these situations are *Acorus*, Butomus, Calla, Calthas, Irises, Lobelia, *Mimulus ringens*, Pontederia, *Sagittaria japonica plena*, *Scirpus albescens*, *Scirpus zebrinus*.

Water-lilies and deep marginals can be planted in a similar fashion in the bottom of the pool. The pockets should be a minimum of 36cm (14in) square or 41cm (16in) diameter, and 15cm (6in) deep. You can make them with sound house bricks or, preferably, ornamental stone blocks. These pockets should be filled with a good heavy soil and topped off with a layer of washed gravel (Fig 55).

I would not advocate constructing pockets for oxygenators as these will thrive in more convenient planting containers.

In Crates and Containers
However, the usual way of planting a pool is by using crates, and the accompanying illustrations show the effect at planting and when established (Figs 56 & 57).

Use a good heavy loam when planting; avoid sandy soil or peat. Probably the best medium is the turf skimmed off when making the pool in a lawn. Remove all the grass if it has not died after being stacked grass side down – two to four weeks in the stack is usually enough. The turves will have a good fibrous root system, and will make an ideal planting medium.

Be careful not to use soil that has been treated with weedkiller or fertilisers (even organic ones). Weedkillers will not only kill the plants but will also harm the fish, as will fertilisers. Soil containing organic fertiliser will cause an excess of algae growth. If plants do require feeding use the special aquatic plant fertiliser, perhaps in the form of tablets.

Planting containers are designed with a lattice open framework. Soil will have a tendency to creep out of the holes at first, so it is better to line the container with hessian or similar material. The hessian will rot away, but by then the plant root system will be binding the soil and very little should escape. Fill the containers to within 13mm (½in) of the surface, levelling off at the top with a layer of washed gravel. Not only does this provide a neat finishing touch; equally important, it prevents the fish from poking and rooting in the soil (Fig 58).

One of the attractions of planting in crates and containers is that you can move the plants around as well as being able to lift them out easily if and when work is needed on the pool. You can thus change the surface appearance

more or less at will, and you have tremendous flexibility as to what and where you plant.

As a rough guide, reckon on needing 2 large containers for water-lilies and 11 or 12 for other plants in a pool of 3·7m² (40sq ft), the smallest practicable. A pool of 11m² (120sq ft) would take 5 large containers and, say, 20 medium. The number of containers used surprises many people; they think little room will be left for the fish to swim! In fact, the containers fit in easily and quickly merge with the surroundings. The 'overcrowding' problem does not really arise, for roughly half the containers are on the marginal shelf and the other half on the bottom of the pool (Fig 59).

A large planting crate is generally recommended for each water-lily, though my own view is that they are not suitable for other than small or medium-growing ones. For large-growing lilies I suggest using plastic containers approximately 38cm (15in) in diameter and 15 to 20cm (6 to 8in) deep. If these are not available, or you have a very large pool, you can make planting pockets on the bottom of the pool (Fig 55). The medium size is suitable for 2 marginals or 12 oxygenating plants or 1 deep marginal plant.

Small crates are not usually recommended except for very small or shallow pools. Like all

Fig 57 The plants have become established and the crates lowered to their correct depth

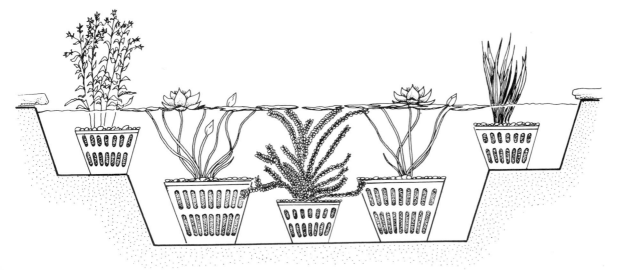

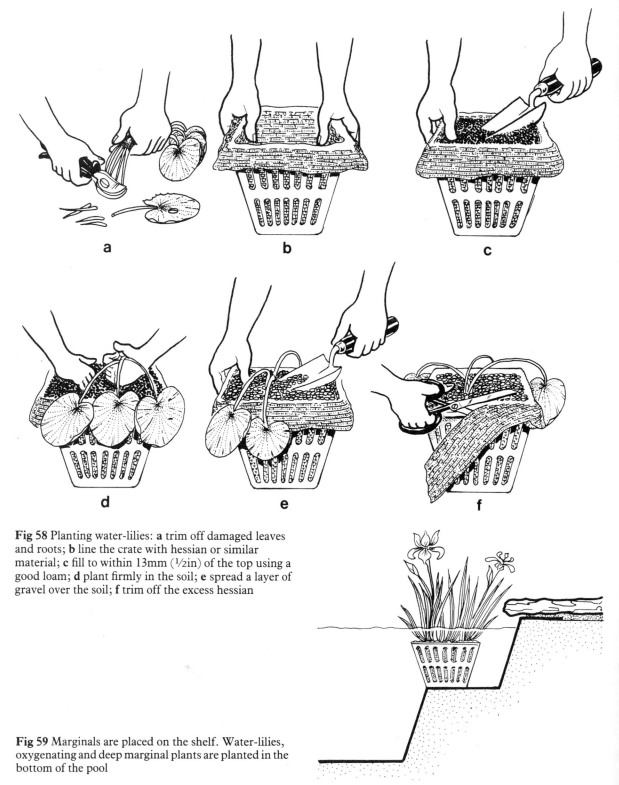

Fig 58 Planting water-lilies: **a** trim off damaged leaves and roots; **b** line the crate with hessian or similar material; **c** fill to within 13mm (½in) of the top using a good loam; **d** plant firmly in the soil; **e** spread a layer of gravel over the soil; **f** trim off the excess hessian

Fig 59 Marginals are placed on the shelf. Water-lilies, oxygenating and deep marginal plants are planted in the bottom of the pool

plants, aquatics can become starved when planted in containers too small for their needs.

PLANTING NATURAL POOLS AND STREAMS

Although nowadays in a comparatively tiny minority of gardens, we cannot ignore natural lakes, pools and streams before leaving the subject of planting. They call for somewhat different treatment. First of all, the weeds will have to be cleared from the banks, margins and the pool itself; otherwise they will quickly destroy any choicer cultivated species that are introduced. In silted-up lakes and ponds, dredging would also be essential before replanting and stocking with fish.

It is far better to take your time in clearing the native vegetation, as the seed and roots can quickly take over again. Regular spraying with a translocated herbicide over a minimum period of twelve months will remove most of the weed infestation. But since aquatic weeds are extremely difficult to control you should consult your local agricultural advisory officer who will be able to advise you on the safest weedkiller to use, particularly in areas where the water runs into streams or open ditches. You can safely use some of these weedkillers where fish are present, but great care must be exercised and the manufacturer's instructions followed to the letter.

Having cleared and cleaned the area of weeds, you are now ready for planting. Plant up the banks and margins with reasonable numbers of plants so that they will soon cover and colonise the open spaces. If you don't, nature will soon take over again with the type of weeds you have just cleared. A list of suitable non-invasive marginals has been given on page 110; for plants for areas above the water-line that have only moist or bog conditions see Chapter 14.

Lilies and deep marginals can be planted directly into the soil, provided the depth of the water is between 15cm (6in) and 1·2m (4ft). A better way however – an adaptation of the con-tainer system already described – is to use wooden boxes such as orange boxes, or old wicker baskets, which are ideal. Fill with good soil and place the plant firmly into this, then set the box approximately 15cm (6in) below the water. When the lily has become established the box can be moved to a permanent position. The box will gradually rot away, and the water-lily will then grow naturally into the soil on the bottom of the pool.

It is highly unlikely that water-lilies and deep-marginal plants would thrive in a stream. However, if there is sufficient depth of water and it is only slow moving, the native British *Nymphaea alba* (true water-lily) could be tried, or the *Nuphar luteum* would possibly be successful.

Natural lakes and pools, however, offer an ideal home for water-lilies and deep-marginal plants; but beware, for some of the latter, and indeed certain varieties of water-lily, can become invasive and take over. Plant in groups leaving open water between varieties, and keep them in check by removing plants that stray. Of the deep marginals Aponogeton, Orontium and Zantedeschia are really the only ones that will not get out of hand.

Regarding floating plants only *Lemna trisulca*, which also doubles as an oxygenator, and *Hydrocharis morsus-ranae* can be safely introduced. *Stratiotes aloides* can also be tried, for if it starts to get out of hand it can be removed reasonably easily. In temperate zones the tropicals can be used even though they are very vigorous growers and quickly spread. The frost will kill them off in the autumn so using them as annuals gives you summer display and interest without fear of their getting out of hand.

Oxygenating plants will also grow rapidly in natural pools, and I am chary of advocating their use there. Far better, I think, to concentrate on planting blocks of water-lilies, or if the water is too deep you could use *Nuphar luteum*, famous for its profusion of small yellow flowers and attractive submerged

leaves. Although oxygenators play an important role in maintaining the ecological balance of a small garden pool, they are not so important in the larger areas and volumes of lakes and natural pools. Here the balance can be maintained by planting bold groups of lilies and deep marginals.

PESTS AND DISEASES
Pests

No garden can ever be entirely free from insect pests of one sort or another, but they do give less trouble in the water garden than elsewhere. There is a ready-made way of getting rid of most of the pests, and that is by keeping fish. In addition other natural predators such as frogs, newts and ladybirds, will help in their control. However, even with fish present, pests can sometimes become a problem. The following are likely to give the most trouble.

Aphids are the universal scourge of gardeners. Several species attack aquatic plants, the worst being the Water-lily Aphid (see Photo 23). The eggs are laid on plum or cherry trees in autumn, and in spring the young aphids fly to whatever is in reach, but show a preference for aquatic plants, with water-lilies the apparent priority. You could use the normal insecticide sprays, but they are toxic; so if fish are present you must pick the aphids off the leaves by hand or wash them off with a hosepipe so that they can be eaten by the fish. Probably a better way is to drown the aphids by submerging the lily leaves, using a piece of sacking or net to weight them down.

The small brown and white China-mark

Photos 23, 24, 25 & 26 Representations of water-lily damage by (top to bottom):
Water-lily aphids
Leaf-mining midge
China-mark Moth larvae
Larvae of the China-mark Moth (inset – actual moth)

118

Moth is a fairly close rival as the number one pool pest (see Photo 25). It is mostly in evidence in mid- to late summer and lays its eggs in clusters near the edges of lily leaves. The eggs hatch into larvae, which cut oval pieces out of the leaf to make a protective covering which they attach to the leaf's underside. As they grow, larger pieces of leaf are cut to form oblong cases 2·5cm (1in) long, which float on the water with the larvae safely inside (see Photo 26). They continue to feed on lily leaves from the protection of this case so it is important to remove them, and this is quite easily done by netting with a small fish net.

The Water-lily Beetle is another specialist concentrating on water-lilies. This creature is the size of a ladybird and arrives in mid-summer, lays eggs in clusters on the leaf surface (in the absence of water-lilies it will attack any suitable plant) and these hatch into small yellowish brown larvae that eat the foliage voraciously. In turn, fish eat the grub-like creatures with relish if they are washed into the water. Control is the same as for aphids. Thorough clearing of dead pool-side vegetation in autumn will also help to control the pest, for this is where the beetles hibernate.

The Caddis Fly is a moth-like insect, and usually visits the pond in the evening to lay its eggs. The larvae build a cylindrical case made up of sticks, sand and pieces of plants as a protective shell. They eat any vegetation within reach and invariably it is not long before fish – notably goldfish and Golden Orfe – make a meal of them. It is unlikely that any other control will be required.

The Leaf-mining Midge is one of the lesser pests, but its presence is quickly noticed. It is the aquatic equivalent of the leaf miner that attacks so many garden plants, tunnelling or furrowing meanderingly through the foliage. In a severe case it can skeletonise the leaf (see Photo 24). The fish should keep it under reasonable control, and they can be helped in this by the removal of heavily infested leaves.

Snails undoubtedly qualify as pests when in great numbers; however, usually they are blamed for damage caused by the pests previously mentioned. Close inspection of the underside of a lily leaf will almost certainly reveal snail eggs, so that when leaves are damaged it is naturally assumed that snails are the cause.

Snails are scavengers, eating decaying plant matter, algae and fish waste, while fish regard their eggs as a delicacy. Normally you need not fear an infestation. Fish eat most of the eggs, and in pools without fish they can easily be removed from the underside of lily leaves where they have been deposited. In addition birds will eat many of the adult snails. If there is a population explosion, snails are very easy to remove with a fish net.

So much for the pests; generally your fish will do a grand job in keeping them down. However, if you do have a severe infestation I suggest you contact a specialist lily grower. These have commercial chemicals for spraying lilies and they will be pleased to assist you.

Diseases

Luckily aquatic plant diseases are very few. Mostly they affect water-lilies although some marginals, notably the Caltha varieties, are prone to mildew. This has little effect, however, and should be ignored. Two forms of leaf-spot affect water-lilies. One causes leaves to dry and crumble at the edges and then apparently disintegrate; the other starts as a dark spot which spreads and destroys the leaves. Another disease of water-lilies mainly attacks the stems, causing them to blacken and rot; and this spreads to the rhizome eventually killing the whole plant.

In each case the treatment is the same. Immediately lift and isolate affected plants in a separate tank, remove and destroy infected leaves, and treat with a fungicide. After treatment the plants must be thoroughly rinsed before returning to the pool.

Most diseases usually follow infestation by

119

the aquatic pests. However, newly planted lilies are especially prone to fungal infections, particularly if planted too deep in the soil or placed under too much water before they are established.

ALGAE

Freshwater algae are microscopic plants of simple structure and are extremely common in all aquatic environments. Although there are hundreds of different species, they can generally be divided into two structural forms. Firstly, there are the free-floating unicellular or small colonial forms which, when present in large numbers, can cause the water to take on a green hue, although red and brown discolorations are not uncommon. Secondly, there are filamentous forms such as blanket weed (*Spirogyra* sp.) which, when aggregated, form cottonwool-like masses which appear on the sides of the pool or over the submerged aquatic plants. It is very unlikely that any pool will be populated with both types. Blanket weed is nearly always associated with pools that have otherwise crystal-clear water.

Algae are not normally hazardous to animal life in the pool, indeed during the day they evolve oxygen which can be used by the animals. In addition they provide an important food source for many pool creatures including fish fry. However, these are small consolations if the ornamental pool acquires an unsightly appearance.

Algal spores are present in all freshwater systems and they grow and multiply at a phenomenal rate in favourable conditions. For survival, they need light, mineral salts and carbon dioxide. The only natural way to control their development in a pool that contains fish is to limit these resources, so starving them out of existence. This is achieved by planting the correct number of aquatic plants

as described on page 101.

A new garden pool will usually turn green due to algal growth despite having the recommended quantities of plant life. This is because the plants have not fully established, and because there is a profusion of mineral salts in the new water and more are dissolving from the new soil used in planting. This situation should soon clear itself, and once a balance is achieved there should be only temporary relapses to a green-water condition. Normally these relapses are associated with seasonal changes, for example warmer weather and higher light intensity in spring and early summer. The pool water should not be changed as this will only destroy the balance that has been developed between the plants and their environment.

There is one other natural method of controlling algae. As mentioned previously, they are an excellent source of food for a wide range of small animals including Daphnia (very small, usually pink crustaceans found in stagnant water and also bought at pet stores) and Tadpoles. The introduction of Daphnia especially to a pool will very soon eliminate algae. Unfortunately if fish are present the Daphnia will very soon be eaten, but they are very useful in pools without fish and in new pools before fish are introduced.

Blanket weed can be removed from a pool with a notched stick or rough piece of wood. If this is poked into the mass and twisted, the blanket weed will wrap around it and can be drawn to the side and removed.

The free-floating algae can be removed by means of a filtration system, although it is unlikely that blanket weed will be affected.

Chemicals are available for treatment of both groups of algae, but should only be considered as a temporary measure and used in conjunction with the natural balance of pool plants.

13 Varieties of Aquatic Plants

HARDY WATER-LILIES (Nymphaeas)
The following abbreviations are used to indicate the relative vigour, planting depth and surface spread of each variety.

(V)	Vigorous variety; planting depth 23–120cm (9–48in); surface spread 1·8–2·3m² (20–25sq ft)
(M-V)	Strong variety; planting depth 23–91cm (9–36in); surface spread 1·3–1·8m² (15–20sq ft)
(M)	Medium variety; planting depth 15–60cm (6–24in); surface spread 1·1–1·3m² (12–15sq ft)
(S-M)	Moderate variety; planting depth 15–45cm (6–18in); surface spread ·6–1·1m² (6–12sq ft)
(S)	Small variety; planting depth 15–38cm (6–15in); surface spread ·3m² (3sq ft)
(T)	Miniature variety; planting depth 10–23cm (4–9in); surface spread ·09m² (1sq ft)

The surface spread is given as a guide only, and indicates the growing potential when planted in containers in the garden pool. If planted in a soil-based pool or in very large containers, the surface spread can be very much greater.

The planting depth is the amount of water above the crown of the lily (see page 104).

White Varieties
alba (V): Perhaps the best-known water-lily, so often does it appear on calendars. Profusion of snow-white flowers, but so vigorous it is not really suitable for small pools.

'Albatross' (M): Large, star-shaped flowers, snow white with golden-yellow anthers. Young foliage purple, maturing to dark green.

candida (S): A small white-flowered variety native to northern Europe. Will thrive even in very cold water.

'Caroliniana nivea' (S): Very fragrant variety for the smaller pool. Pure white blooms are large for the growth habit.

'Gladstoniana' (V): Largest of the whites, fragrant flowers up to 25cm (10in) across. Only suitable for very large pools.

'Gonnêre' (S-M): Large, double, snow-white flowers; outer petal conspicuously stained and striped green. Centre of flower well-filled with golden-yellow anthers.

'Marliacea Albida' (M): Strong growing and free flowering, with large white flowers. Dark-green foliage; fragrant. A most reliable variety suitable for medium-large pools.

odorata 'Alba' (M): Pure-white, cup-shaped scented blooms, free-flowering variety with bright apple-green foliage.

pygmaea 'Alba' (T): Smallest of the whites; small star-shaped flowers, rounded light-green foliage. Ideal for shallow pools, tubs and sinks.

tuberosa 'Richardsonii' (M-V): Large globular flowers, snow white with conspicuous pea-green sepals. Golden-yellow stamens.

Pink Varieties
'Amabilis' (M): Beautiful star-shaped flowers from salmon to deep pink, shaded white; orange stamens; purple foliage turning green.

'Brackleyi Rosea' (M-V): Prolifically flowering;

beautifully perfumed blooms of deep rose which pale with age.

'**Colossea**' (V): Enormous flowers, blush-pink to white, blooming in abundance throughout summer. One of the finest varieties for very large pools.

'**Firecrest**' (S-M): Always considered one of the finest pinks. Deep-pink scented flowers with orange-red stamens (see page 93).

'**Laydekeri Lilacea**' (T): A variety suitable for shallow pools or tub cultivation. Scented, soft rose-pink flowers.

'**Marliacea Carnea**' (M-V): Exceptionally strong growing, pretty shade of blush white, stained rose towards base of flower (see page 94).

'**Marliacea Rosea**' (M): Very similar to **carnea** only slightly deeper pink. Usually flowers white for the first year or so.

'**Mme Wilfron Gonnère**' (M): One of the few water-lilies that has double flowers. Beautiful blooms of soft-pink flushed white.

'**Mrs Richmond**' (M): Huge, pale rose-pink flowers on opening which deepen with age; light-green foliage.

odorata '**Eugenia de Land**' (S-M): Ideal variety for the small pool. Medium-sized star-shaped flowers in a delightful shade of rich pink.

odorata '**W. B. Shaw**' (S-M): Delightfully scented variety; large cup-shaped flowers with narrow pointed petals in a pretty shade of shell pink.

'**Pink Opal**' (M): Star-shaped flowers a pretty shade of coral pink, standing above the water level.

'**Rose Arey**' (S-M): Cerise-pink scented flowers with incurving petals; brilliant orange stamens, tipped yellow; purple leaves turning to green.

tuberosa '**Rosea**' (M): Very fragrant medium-sized flowers of soft pink, shaded white; strong growing; bright-green foliage.

Red Varieties

'**Attraction**' (M): A glowing shade of garnet red, tipped with white flecks; free flowering (see page 93).

'**Charles de Meurville**' (M-V): Large wine-red flowers, up to 25cm (10in) across. Early to bloom; long flowering season.

'**Conqueror**' (M-V): Large well-formed blooms, mainly blood red, flecked white; stays open in the evening.

'**Ellisiana**' (S): Excellent variety with small, dark vermilion-red flowers and olive-green foliage.

'**Escarboucle**' (M): The most outstanding red variety; large blooms of intense vermilion crimson, free flowering and long lasting.

'**Froebeli**' (S): Fragrant blood-red flowers, olive-green foliage. A free-flowering and reliable small red.

'**James Brydon**' (S-M): Peony-type flowers of pink crimson; leaves purple, turning to dark green. One of the finest water-lilies in cultivation.

'**Laydekeri Purpurata**' (T): A good red for small pools or for tub culture. Wine-red, slightly spotted white, star-shaped flowers.

pygmaea '**Rubra**' (T): Slightly smaller than **Laydekeri**. Opens deep pink and ages to dark red. True miniature for very small pools, tubs or bowls.

'**René Gerrard**' (M): Very free flowering when established. Rich rose colour splashed with red.

'**William Falconer**' (M): Very dark-red star-shaped flowers 15–18cm (6–7in) across with golden anthers; purple leaves changing to dark green.

Yellow Varieties

'**Charlene Strawn**' (M): A recent cultivar from the USA. Golden-yellow flowers held above the surface, more like a tropical variety.

'**Colonel A. J. Welch**' (V): Vigorous canary-yellow, large flowers which stand well out of the water. Not very free flowering, but will grow in deeper water than the other yellows.

Photo 27 *Eichhornia crassipes*

'**Marliacea Chromatella**' (M): Deservedly one of the most popular of all hardy lilies. The large well-shaped flowers are a delightful shade of soft glistening yellow; dark-green foliage mottled and spotted reddish brown. Free flowering.

'**Moorei**' (M): Very similar to **chromatella**, but the primrose-yellow flowers are slightly more distinct. Foliage spotted purple on underside.

odorata '**Sulphurea Grandiflora**' (M): Like '**Sunrise**' it prefers a warmer climate. Narrower and more numerous petals than most varieties; golden-yellow colour, shy bloomer (see page 94).

pygmaea '**Helvola**' (T): Dainty canary-yellow star-shaped flowers with orange stamens, very free flowering throughout the summer. Small, round green leaves heavily mottled with purple and brown. Ideal for growing in a bowl, tub or very small pool.

'**Sunrise**' (M): Rivalling the tropicals in glory, but without the problems. Huge golden blooms, enhanced by the bright golden-yellow filaments. To flower to its full potential it needs a warmer climate than most of the hardy types.

Copper and Changeable Varieties

These varieties change colour with age and are difficult to classify. All have mottled foliage.

'**Aurora**' (S): Remarkable for its changes of colour. Opens a pretty shade of copper yellow turning to salmon orange and then ruby red. Foliage prettily marbled. Very free flowering.

'**Comanche**' (S-M): Copper yellow shading towards orange scarlet; stamens a deep orange-red – a pleasing combination of shades.

'**Indiana**' (S): Frequently changes colour, going from orange yellow to red bronze and finally to copper red; foliage green, spotted maroon. Free flowering.

'**Paul Hariot**' (S): Abundant flowering; opening yellow flushed rose, deepening to copper red; foliage green, spotted maroon.

'**Robinsoniana**' (S): Predominant colour vermilion, but shaded orange towards centre.

Large flowers in comparison to the foliage.

'**Sioux**' (S-M): Changes colour often, varying buff yellow to orange and peach. Foliage a fairly static olive green slightly spotted purple.

TROPICAL WATER-LILIES

There are so many varieties, and new ones are introduced frequently, that it is only possible to list a small selection here. Tropicals are not easy to obtain in Britain as they are rarely successful, even with growers. In warmer climates they are more easily available, although many suppliers consider them more as annual plants to be replaced each season.

They should be planted with 15–20cm (6–8in) of water over the crown.

White

ampla (specie): Very free flowering, medium-sized star-shaped blooms.

'**Mrs George H. Pring**': Large flowers; speckled foliage; very fragrant.

Yellow

'**Aviator Pring**': Deep-yellow blooms; mottled leaves.

'**St Louis**': Large blooms; well-speckled foliage. Thrives in moderate sunlight.

Blue

'**Blue Beauty**': Large deep-blue fragrant flowers, golden/violet stamens; large leaves.

'**Bob Trickett**': Huge deep-blue cup-shaped flowers, sometimes 30cm (12in) in diameter.

'**Colorate**': Small bluish-purple blooms; pygmy type.

'**Dauben**': Prolific; small, scented blooms, often a number out at once. Tolerates less sun than most tropicals.

'**Mrs Martin Randig**': Medium-sized blooms. Adaptable to tub gardening – a half beer barrel (or wine cask) half filled with soil and topped up with 20cm (8in) of water.

Pink

'**General Pershing**': Double pink blooms 20cm

(8in) across; probably the finest pink of the day-blooming tropicals.

'**Pink Platter**': Many-petalled, medium-pink blooms; flowers profusely.

Purple
'**Director George T. Moore**': Clusters of deep, rich-purple flowers, golden centred.
'**Panama Pacific**': Deep purple-blue flowers, turning reddish purple; free flowering.

Night Blooming
'**Emily Hutchings**': Clusters of deep-rose blooms, coppery-bronze foliage.
'**H. C. Haarstick**': Fragrant deep pink/red blooms, copper foliage.
'**Missouri**': Giant white flowers; very large mottled-green foliage.
'**Mrs George C. Hitchcock**': Rose-pink flowers, probably the largest of this type, often exceeding 30cm (12in) in diameter; deep-red foliage.

OXYGENATING PLANTS
Callitriche autumnalis: An excellent oxygenator, one of the few submerged aquatics that are active during the winter months.
Callitriche verna (Water Starwort): Dense tufts of light-green underwater foliage, rising to the surface during summer, providing shade and protection for fish.
Ceratophyllum demersum: An oxygenating aquatic that never reaches the surface; fragile branching stems, with dense whorls of spiny foliage.
Eleocharis acicularis (Hair-grass): Dense mats of hair-like foliage, giving a very graceful effect under water.
Elodea canadensis (**Anacharis** canadensis): An excellent oxygenator, but must be kept in check owing to its rampant propagation.
Fontinalis antipyretica (Willow Moss): Congested bunches of branching stems covered with short moss-like foliage; an invaluable plant for pool or stream.
Hottonia palustris (Water Violet): A charm-

Photo 28 *Scirpus zebrinus*

125

ing plant; one of the few oxygenating aquatics to produce flowers. Stems have many whorls of delicate green fern-like foliage; from the centre of top whorl, stem protrudes 15–30cm (6–12in) above water level bearing lovely violet-like flowers varying in colour from white to lavender.

Lagarosiphon major (Elodea crispa): A very distinct variety; ascending stems densely clothed with narrow reflexed leaves; good oxygenator.

Myriophyllum spicatum: Whorls of finely cut bronze-green foliage.

Myriophyllum verticillatum: Densely clothed with whorls of divided rich-green foliage.

Potamogeton crispus: Prettily crimped foliage, dark green, passing to bronze.

Ranunculus aquatilis (Water Buttercup): Pretty submerged plant with distinctive foliage; underwater the leaves are finely cut, surface foliage small clover-shaped leaves; snow-white flowers 2·5cm (1in) above water.

Tillaea recurva: One of the finest submerged oxygenating aquatics; when established is a dense green carpet, thriving in water varying in depth from a few inches to 1m (3ft). A good 'green-food' for fish; keeps its bright-green character throughout winter months.

FLOATING PLANTS

Azolla caroliniana (Fairy Moss): Delightful little floating plant, ideal for pool or aquarium; dense carpets of pale-green fern-like foliage, which in late summer and autumn assumes a bright reddish tint; do not introduce into lakes or large pools.

Eichhornia crassipes (Water Hyacinth): One of the most beautiful aquatics. Bases of the handsome shiny foliage form floats which support the plant and give it buoyancy, whilst bunches of feathery roots grow into the water and enable the plant to flourish and flower without the aid of soil. Has lovely lavender-blue flowers, conspicuously illuminated by a purple peacock eye, produced in late summer; in dull and rainy summers failing to flower. Invaluable for fish breeding, goldfish in particular depositing their eggs among its feathery roots (not hardy) (see Photo 27).

Hydrocharis morsus-ranae (Frog-bit): Rosettes of bright-green leaves; small snow-white flowers, closely resembling a tiny water-lily. One of the finest hardy floating subjects.

Lemna gibba (Thick Duckweed): Bright-green disc-like, almost spherical fronds 3mm (⅛in) diameter. Rampant growing; do not introduce into large pools or lakes.

Lemna minor (Lesser Duckweed): Commonest of all duckweeds; excellent food for fish in both pool and aquarium; very rampant; do not introduce into lakes or large pools.

Lemna polyrrhiza (Greater Duckweed): Large leaves, green and maroon nearly 1·3cm (½in) in diameter. Not as rampant as **gibba** or **minor**, but should not be introduced into lakes.

Lemna trisulca (Ivy-leaved Duckweed): The prettiest of the species. Light-green transparent fronds; an excellent plant for maintaining clear water.

Pistia stratiotes (Water Lettuce): Very graceful floating plant for indoor aquarium or outside pool during summer months. Bold rosettes of pale-green hairy foliage, with long white feathery roots; ideal for spawning fish (not hardy).

Salvinia braziliensis: Decorative floating aquatic with dainty pea-green leaves, covered with velvety nap of silky hairs (not hardy).

Stratiotes aloides (Water Soldier): Curious floating plant closely resembling spiny foliage of a pineapple. Lies submerged for considerable period, rising to surface during summer months in which the white flowers are produced.

Trapa natans (Water Chestnut): A beautiful floating plant for aquarium or garden pool. From a curiously formed nut, thin stems issue, terminating in huge rosettes of olive-green foliage and small pure-white flowers (not hardy).

Utricularia vulgaris (Bladderwort): Most interesting insectivorous plant for aquarium or pool. (Its small egg-shaped bladders have a valve-type entry triggered by bristles on the aperture. Once activated, the insect prey is sucked into the bladders.) Floats on the surface and produces clusters of dainty bright-yellow flowers raised a few inches above water. After blooming, plant submerges.

MARGINAL PLANTS

The average height for an established plant is shown against each variety in the list. The depth refers to the amount of water above the soil (see page 109).

Acorus calamus (Sweet-scented Rush): Strong growing iris-like rush with dark-green aromatic foliage. Height 76cm (2½ft); depth 8–12cm (3–5in).

Acorus calamus variegatus: Beautiful variegated variety; bold, sword-like foliage, rich green, conspicuously lined white; one of the most effective poolside plants. Height 76cm (2½ft); depth 8–12cm (3–5in).

Acorus gramineus: Neat tufts of thin grass-like foliage, standing 15cm (6in) above water level; a pretty species. Height 15–23cm (6–9in); depth 0–8cm (0–3in).

Acorus gramineus variegatus: Close tufts of dark-green grass-like foliage suffused and striped sulphur yellow. Height 15–23cm (6–9in); depth 0–8cm (0–3in).

Alisma parviflora: Pretty rounded foliage, small rose-white flowers; a distinct North American species. Height 46cm (1½ft); depth 0–8cm (0–3in).

Alisma plantago: Attractive ovate foliage; loose pyramidal panicles, bearing a profusion of small rose and white flowers. Height 60cm (2ft); depth 0–12cm (0–5in).

Butomus umbellatus (Flowering Rush): One of the most beautiful native British aquatics; green triangular foliage; bold leafless stems terminating in large umbels of rose-coloured flowers. Height 76cm (2½ft); depth 8–12cm (3–5in).

Calla palustris (Bog Arum): Bright-green cordate foliage; white arum-like flowers, succeeded by crimson-coloured fruits; creeping habit. Height 23cm (9in); depth 5–10cm (2–4in).

Caltha palustris (Marsh Marigold or Kingcup): Bold tufts of dark-green foliage; stout branching stems bearing profusion of brilliant golden-yellow flowers in early spring and summer. Height 38cm (15in); depth 0–8cm (0–3in).

Caltha palustris 'Alba': Small white flowers; a charming form introduced from Himalayas. Height 30cm (1ft); depth 0–5cm (0–2in).

Caltha palustris plena: One of the finest marginal plants. Very attractive spring-flowering variety; masses of dark olive-green foliage; large, double, golden-yellow flowers. Height 30cm (12in); depth 0–5cm (0–2in).

Caltha polypetala: Attractive, large, dark-green leaves and profusion of golden-yellow flowers. Height 60–90cm (2–3ft); depth 0–12cm (0–5in) (see page 36).

Carex stricta 'Bowles Golden': Very decorative variety for shallow water or wet soil; foliage rich golden-yellow; one of the most effective water grasses. Height 38cm (15in); depth 0–8cm (0–3in).

Cotula coronopifolia (Golden Buttons): Excellent for small or large pools: covered throughout summer and even into early winter with small yellow button-like flowers. Height 23cm (9in); depth 0–12cm (0–5in).

Cyperus alternifolius: Very pretty species; tall stems terminating in heads of rich-green leaves. One of most decorative of this genus, can be successfully grown in shallow water. Height 76cm (2½ft); depth 0–5cm (0–2in) – (not hardy).

Cyperus gracilis: Dwarf and distinct; slender wire-like stems terminating in loose flower-heads of long leaf-like bracts forming fluffy brown heads. Height 46cm (1½ft); depth 0–5cm (0–2in) – (not hardy).

Cyperus longus (sweet or English Galingale): Close tufts of grass-like foliage terminating in

Photo 29 *Typha minima*

reddish-brown heads. One of the most decorative British species: perfectly hardy and useful for cutting. Height 76cm (2½ft); depth 8–12cm (3–5in).

Cyperus papyrus (Egyptian Paper-rush): Stout stems terminating in crowded tufts of long thread-like leaves. Ancient paper-plant both interesting and decorative; when established attains height of 3m (10ft); depth 0–5cm (0–2in) – (not hardy).

Cyperus vegetus: Broad grass-like foliage and crowded umbels of mahogany-coloured flowers; in character throughout the winter months. Height 60cm (2ft); depth 0–10cm (0–4in).

Eriophorum angustifolium (Cotton Grass): Attractive low-growing perennial; neat tufts of rush-like foliage with numerous slender stems terminating in globular heads of snow-white silky tufts. Height 30cm (12in); depth 0–5cm (0–2in) (see page 36).

Eriophorum latifolium: Very similar to **angustifolium** but with several drooping spikelets to each stem. Height 38cm (15in); depth 0–5cm (0–2in).

Glyceria spectabilis variegata: One of most beautiful variegated grasses; graceful foliage, regularly striped white, yellow and green, tinted rose during spring and early summer. Height 60cm (2ft); depth 8–12cm (3–5in).

Hippuris vulgaris: Simple stems, upper part projecting 15–23cm (6–9in) above water, whole length whorled with short linear leaves; good subject for running water. Curious water perennial found throughout Europe, Asia and America; can be difficult to control. Height 38cm (15in); depth 8–25cm (3–10in).

Houttuynia cordata: Japanese perennial possessing a charm of its own; pretty red stems; blue-green heart-shaped foliage illuminated by four snow-white bracts and conspicuous

Page 129 (above) Sarasa Comet; *(below)* Blue Comet Shubunkin

cone of modest flowers. Height 30cm (12in); depth 0–10cm (0–4in).

Houttuynia cordata plena: Double and more pleasing form of above. Height 30cm (12in); depth 0–10cm (0–4in).

Iris laevigata: Smooth green foliage from which issue numerous stems bearing large brilliant violet-blue flowers at intervals from June until September. One of the most beautiful water-loving species in cultivation; native of Japan. Height 60cm (2ft); depth 5–10cm (2–4in).

Iris laevigata Mottled Beauty: Standards of this variety are creamy-white, the well-developed falls are white flecked with pale-blue blotches. Height 60cm (2ft); depth 5–10cm (2–4in).

Iris laevigata 'Rose Queen': One of the loveliest waterside plants, ideal for shallow water or damp soil; handsome grass-like foliage; dainty rose-coloured flowers. Height 60cm (2ft); depth 0–2·5cm (0–1in).

Iris laevigata 'Snowdrift': Largest flowering water-iris; pure-white flowers with six dainty heart-shaped petals attractively marbled yellow at base (see Photo 30). Height 60cm (2ft); depth 5–10cm (2–4in).

Iris laevigata 'Variegata': One of the most beautiful of all aquatic irises; fan-shaped green and white foliage; very dainty blue flowers. Height 60cm (2ft); depth 0–8cm (0–3in).

Iris pseudacorus (Yellow Water Flag): Vigorous-growing species, stately foliage, not suitable for small garden pools; flowers deep yellow. Height 1–1·2m (3–4ft); depth 8–12cm (3–5in).

Iris pseudacorus 'Variegata' (Variegated Water Iris): One of the most attractive water-garden plants, especially during spring and early summer when foliage is bright golden; from mid-summer onwards leaves become flecked with green, assuming a complete dark

green as autumn approaches; bright golden-yellow flowers. Height 76cm (2½ft); depth 8–12cm (3–5in).

Iris versicolor: Distinctive variegated blooms of rich blue and yellow. Height 46cm (1½ft); depth 5–10cm (2–4in).

Iris versicolor 'Kermesina': Variegated flowers of rich claret, speckled yellow. Height 46cm (1½ft); depth 5–10cm (2–4in).

Juncus effusus 'Spiralis' (Corkscrew Rush): More curious than pretty, each stem is spirally twisted after manner of corkscrew. Height 46cm (1½ft); depth 8–12cm (3–5in).

Lobelia cardinalis: Not usually thought of as an aquatic subject. Striking plant with crimson foliage and stems; brilliant red flowers. Height 60cm (2ft); depth 0–8cm (0–3in).

Lysimachia nummularia: Dense carpets of bright-green foliage, covered with golden-yellow flowers. Height 15cm (6in); depth 8–12cm (3–5in).

Mentha aquatica (Water Mint): Aromatic foliage; clustered heads of lilac-coloured flowers. Height 38cm (15in); depth 5–10cm (2–4in).

Menyanthes trifoliata (Bog Bean): A most desirable species for shallow water; strong, creeping rootstock, attractive three-leaved foliage and delicate rose-pink and white flowers. Height 23cm (9in); depth 8–12cm (3–5in).

Mimulus 'Hose-in-Hose': Stiff stems terminating in loose heads of brilliant yellow, semi-double flowers. Height 46cm (1½ft); depth 0–5cm (0–2in).

Mimulus luteus (Monkey Musk): Close tufts of hairy foliage from which arise stiff stems bearing profusion of rich golden-yellow flowers throughout summer months. Height 46cm (1½ft); depth 0–5cm (0–2in).

Mimulus ringens: Close tufts of dark-green foliage; stout stems terminating in clustered spikes of soft-blue flowers; a gem for shallow water. Height 46cm (1½ft); depth 5–12cm (2–5in).

Myosotis palustris (Water Forget-me-not): A most delightful little plant for growing in a few

Page 130 (above) Golden Orfe; *(below)* Common Goldfish

Photo 30 *Iris laevigata* Snowdrift

inches of water; attractive light-green foliage; flowers clear blue with small yellow eye. Height 23cm (9in); depth 0–8cm (0–3in).

Myriophyllum prosderpinacoides (Parrot's Feather): Attractive creeping subject with bright-green, feathery foliage held 15–23cm (6–9in) above water level; depth 8–12cm (3–5in).

Pontederia cordata (Pickerel Weed): Attractive lanceolate leaves borne on long stiff stems; numerous spikes of light-blue flowers conspicuously spotted green; summer and autumn flowering. Height 60cm (2ft); depth 8–12cm (3–5in).

Ranunculus lingua grandiflora (Great Spearwort): Erect, hollow stems well clothed with narrow dark-green leaves; golden-yellow flowers, all summer; reminiscent of a giant buttercup. Height 60cm (2ft); depth 5–15cm (2–6in).

Ranunculus flammula: Attractive variety with small yellow flowers. Height 30cm (1ft); depth 0–8cm (0–3in).

Sagittaria japonica (Arrowhead): Bold sagittate foliage; slender stems bearing profusion of large snow-white flowers in July or August; very attractive species. Height 76cm (2½ft); depth 8–12cm (3–5in).

Sagittaria japonica 'Flore Pleno': Attractive foliage; bold spikes bearing a profusion of double snow-white flowers; one of the finest aquatics. Height 60cm (2ft); depth 8–12cm (3–5in) (see page 112).

Sagittaria sagittifolia (Common Arrowhead): Arrow-shaped leaves rising out of water; erect stems bearing several whorls of snow-white flowers in late summer. Height 46cm (1½ft); depth 8–12cm (3–5in).

Saururus cernuus (American Swamp Lily): Slender stems well clothed with dark-green heart-shaped foliage; terminal sprays of nodding creamy-white flowers; summer flowering. Height 46cm (1½ft); depth 0–10cm (0–4in).

Scirpus 'Albescens': Very attractive vertical stripes of green and cream on cylindrical stems. Height 1·1m (3½ft); depth 8–12cm (3–5in) (see page 76).

Scirpus lacustris (True Bullrush): Bold cylindrical stems. (Does not have poker-heads – see **Typha**.) Can be invasive and difficult to control. Height 1·5–1·8m (5–6ft); depth 8–12cm (3–5in).

Scirpus 'Zebrinus' (Zebra Rush): Bold clumps of porcupine-quill foliage, transversely banded with white and green; when established one of the most attractive grasses in cultivation (see Photo 28). Height 1m (3ft); depth 8–12cm (3–5in).

Typha angustifolia: Variable species with narrow glaucous foliage; narrow brown poker-heads in autumn; strong grower, invasive. Height 1–1·2m (3–4ft); depth 8–15cm (3–6in).

Typha latifolia (Great Reedmace): Often incorrectly termed 'bullrush', broad linear foliage, stout stems terminating in bold poker-heads of rusty-brown cat's-tail-like inflorescence; strong grower, invasive. Height 1·5–1·8m (5–6ft); depth 8–30cm (3–12in).

Typha minima; Narrow rush-like foliage; diminutive brown inflorescence; a fine subject for small pools – plant in shallow water (see Photo 29). Height 46cm (1½ft); depth 5–12cm (2–5in).

Veronica beccabunga (Brooklime): Olive-green foliage and light-blue flowers; creeping habit. Height 15cm (6in); depth 0–10cm (0–4in).

DEEP MARGINALS

Aponogeton distachyum (Water Hawthorn): Strap-shaped leaves, and white flowers with contrasting black stamens floating on the water, make this one of loveliest of all water plants. Blooms throughout spring and early summer, then dies back in June and July only to gather strength to bloom again from August until early winter; has even been known to be still blooming at Christmas. Has a delightful vanilla fragrance (see Photo 31). Planting depth 15–76cm (6–30in), but should be started at only 15cm (6in).

Nuphar luteum (Brandy Bottle or Yellow Water-lily): Often seen in large lakes, but too vigorous for ordinary water gardens. Probably at its best in natural conditions, for it tolerates slow-moving water and is very successful in water too deep or too shaded for the true water-lily, which it resembles. Small yellow flowers; planting depth ·3–1·8m (1–6ft).

Nymphoides peltata (Villarsia or Water Fringe): Leaves like a small water-lily 10–12cm (4–5in) across; dainty yellow flowers. Very fast-spreading habit, making it ideal for new pools because it soon affords surface cover while you wait for water-lilies to establish. Planting depth 10–46cm (4–18in).

Orontium aquaticum (Golden Club): One of

133

Photo 31 *Aponogeton distachyum*

the most attractive aquatics. Yellow flower on a poker-like white stem; sturdy leaves have silvery metallic bluish-green sheen and stand out of water or lie on surface; needs a large planting crate for best results. Sometimes listed as a marginal; start it on marginal shelf and lower it as it establishes. Planting depth 8–30cm (3–12in) (see page 112).

Sagittaria natans: Small strap-like leaves with correspondingly small white flowers. Appear-ance is of some interest, but it cannot compare with **Aponogeton** and is not particularly recommended except perhaps as a contrast. Planting depth 15–46cm (6–18in).

Zantedeschia aethiopica (Arum Lily): Not usually thought of as aquatic plant, but worthy of a place in any pool. The attractive crinkled leaves stand well out of the water, as do the magnificent white flowers (correctly known as spathes). Start it on marginal shelf in 2·5–5cm (1–2in) of water and gradually lower it as it establishes. Will overwinter in the pool, surviving frosts if 15cm (6in) below water level. Planting depth 15–30cm (6–12in).

14 The Bog and Moisture Garden

The moisture-loving plants are the 'odd men out' of the water garden, as it can be argued that they are not strictly pool plants. However, they can form a very attractive feature in any garden that can provide the right conditions. As the name indicates, they grow at the sides of natural pools (not actually in the water), where they thrive in the moist environment. In natural pools they are very much at home, but with man-made pools it is unlikely that there will be the natural conditions to suit them unless a special area has been incorporated at the design stage. Bog or moisture conditions can be man-made in any part of the garden and it follows that a pool is not essential. However, such a garden does make an ideal partner to a pool, forming a natural 'buffer state' between the pool and the rest of the garden, presenting a gradual transformation.

A bog, by definition, is a wet or swampy area where only certain species of plants, adapted to these conditions, will grow. There will be little air in the soil, as it will have been displaced by water. Many of the marginal plants listed previously can be classed as bog plants and will thrive in these conditions, beside other bog subjects. A distinction must be made here between the bog subjects and those plants which require only moist conditions. Moisture-loving plants occupy the higher levels of the bog area where there is more air than water in the soil, but the water level is not far below the surface so that they always have moisture available at their roots. A point to remember is that bog plants will adapt and grow on the higher ground, but moisture plants will not tolerate bog or waterlogged conditions. Unless you have these natural conditions, you will have to manufacture them.

BOG-GARDEN CONSTRUCTION
The method of construction of the bog garden will have a familiar ring – dig out the area required as though excavating for a pool, and store the soil conveniently nearby. You will need to dig at least 30cm (12in) deep and slope the base.

Photo 32 *Primula bullevana*

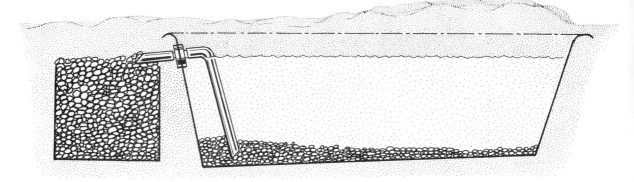

Fig 60 A typical bog-garden construction showing the liner and overflow system

It is essential to arrange for some form of drainage to avoid a build-up of sour soil caused by stagnant water. Line the excavation, but not so meticulously as you did for the pool – a cheaper or secondhand liner will do for this task. With the liner in place, cover the bottom with a layer of gravel. Fit a special inlet fitting of 2·5cm (1in) bore minimum through the liner 15 to 23cm (6 to 9in) below ground level; connect a reinforced hose from this to the lowest point inside the bog, and cover with gravel. The outlet side needs a hose-fitting leading to a soakaway or drain. The outlet pipe will determine the water level within the bog, so it must be laid with this important factor in mind (Fig 60). It will remove stagnant water from the bottom as fresh water from irrigation, or rain, filters through; it will also provide an artificial water level 15 to 23cm (6 to 9in) below ground level.

Before you fill the bog garden, the soil should be well mixed with peat, humus, leaf mould and any other enriching substance you can find. Chopped-up turf will also do admirably, but keep as much of the topsoil as you can for the final layer. You will need to add fresh water from time to time particularly in dry spells, and it is a good idea to run a double length of old hose about 8cm (3in) below the surface. There should be a number of slits or holes in it, the idea being to provide a type of trickle-irrigation system. Cap one end and leave the other available but not too well exposed, for fixing to the garden hose. Planting levels can vary to suit the different types of plant. As already mentioned, those requiring boggy conditions will be on the lower levels and those needing only moist conditions will be planted higher.

A bog garden can be linked to the main pool by extending the marginal shelf to cover the area required. (Allow for this extra dimension when ordering your liner.) When the liner is fitted the two are separated by laying stones bedded on mortar (3–1 sand/cement mix) across the back of the marginal shelf. This principle can also be used round the outer edge of the bog garden, the liner being brought up behind these stones; but make sure the liner level is above that of the water, otherwise there will be seepage. Fill in the area of bog garden with a good rich fibrous loam 8 to 15cm (3 to 6in) above the water level and plant with your selected plants. This is a simple way to make an unusual and very attractive extension to your pool, extending the range and number of plants that can be grown (Fig 61).

MOISTURE-GARDEN CONSTRUCTION

Moisture-loving plants need only be assured of sufficient moisture at their roots in the growing season. They can be grown on the raised area of the bog garden, where the crown of the plant is in normal conditions but its roots have access to moisture. In the orthodox garden this condition can be achieved by adding plenty of humus to the soil – peat, leaf mould, bark, etc – and by arranging an irrigation supply for the summer months. Sub-irrigation at around root level is best.

If the soil is very light and drains quickly you can still provide for moisture-loving plants by laying a liner of polythene, PVC or butyl a minimum of 30cm (12in) below ground level with the sides turned up 5–8cm (2 to 3in) to form a shallow trough. This will stop the otherwise rapid drainage, and allow the soil and roots time to absorb the water. Even the big spectacular rhubarb-like plants such as Gunnera and Rheum, planted round the edge, will be able to send down their deep-feeding roots and thrive (Fig 62).

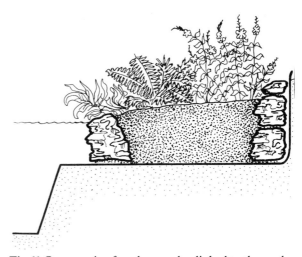

Fig 61 Construction for a bog garden linked to the pool

RANGE OF PLANTS

Though we talk about 'marginal plants' and 'bog plants', this is really an artificial distinction, for most of the marginals are bog plants and can be grown in the bog garden. They do not have to be submerged and will thrive in bog conditions, but avoid any varieties that may be invasive.

All Calthas grow well in these conditions, as will the Acorus. Eriophorum, Glyceria and Cyperus will all thrive, but they should be kept in check and stopped from spreading. The Scirpus – *albescens* and *zebrinus* – make striking plants in these situations, whilst Houttuynia will provide good ground cover. All the Irises mentioned in the marginal section are suitable and will not become invasive.

There is an enormous range of other appropriate plants for the waterside area and a good nursery or specialist catalogue will list hundreds from which to choose. The following list is merely a taster, but selection from it will provide a good all-round display of flower and foliage. As a guide to the conditions required, all plants listed are followed by the letter (B)

Fig 62 The needs of moisture-loving plants can be provided by using a liner to retain water

137

Photo 33 *Hemerocallis*, the day lily

for true bog plants or (M) for plants that are moisture loving.

Astilbes (M): Come in a great number of varieties, their graceful plumes appearing in various shades of red, pink, white or cream, all augmented by handsome foliage. Most grow to about ·7m (2½ft) and flower from June onwards.

Gunnera manicata (M): Only suitable for large gardens; makes a large and impressive specimen with spiky stem and leaves up to 3m (10ft) high and 2·4m (8ft) across. Flower

spike, up to 1m (3ft) long, is like a bottle-brush turning rusty brown.

Hemerocallis (Day Lily) (M): Deservedly popular for its attractive lily-like flowers which last for barely a day but follow on in abundance giving a spectacular display (see Photo 33). The many varieties, ranging in height from ·5–1·5m (1½–5ft), flower from June to September; colours mainly yellow, apricot, orange or pink. The mixed collections are probably the best buy.

Hosta (M): The plantain lilies are fine foliage plants, invaluable for poolside planting; handsome leaves in various shades of green, many with white or yellow variegation. Most produce arching spikes of lavender-blue flowers from June to August. Height around ·5–·7m (1½–2½ft); also do extremely well in shade.

Iris: There are many varieties suitable for the bog or moisture garden; two forms are especially noteworthy:

I. kaempferi (B & M) is magnificent in these conditions; the leaves have an easily distinguishable midrib, helping to identify them (see Photo 34). Originating from Japan, they grow to between ·7–1m (2½–3½ft) high with spectacular giant blooms up to 25cm (10in) across, mostly in variations of blue, purple, rose, white and variegated blooms including many double forms. Known as clematis-flowered because of the almost horizontal angle of the lower petals or falls; make a spectacular splash of colour. Some outstanding varieties are: 'Blue Peter', large double, rich Oxford-blue flowers 18cm (7in) across; 'Apollo', large double white flower, shading to pale yellow at throat; 'Higo Selected', mixed pastel shades, single and double flowers up to 25cm (10in) across; 'Hokaido', medium-sized single pale-blue flowers veined reddish maroon; 'Mandarin', double flowers of rich purple violet assuming a striking reddish glow with age; 'Variegata', striking green and white foliage, rich-purple flowers.

I. sibirica (B & M) has less spectacular markings and flowers. Of central European

Photo 34 *Iris kaempferi*

origin, in general it grows slightly taller, up to 1·2m (4ft), although there are dwarfer varieties. Colour variation mainly purple, blue and white with attractive grassy foliage. Varieties well worth growing include: 'Blue King', rich purple-blue flowers; 'Emperor', large violet-blue flowers; 'Marcus Perry', large rich-blue flowers; 'Mrs Rowe', dainty pale-lilac flowers; 'Perry's Favourite', lavender blue, falls rich violet with conspicuous white crest; 'Perry's Pygmy', deep-blue flowers; 'Snow Queen', flowers white with yellow centre.

A good supplier can offer at least ten or a dozen varieties of each of the two forms, so there is ample choice. Though flowering times

Photo 35 A pool-side scene with *Trollius* in the foreground

do overlap, as a rough guide the sibiricas are at their best in June/July and the kaempferis later in July. Mix good clumps of each and you will get a wonderful water's edge display for nearly three months.

Lobelia (M & B): Best known as annual or perennial for the herbaceous border, but some varieties well suited to the waterside and have additional virtue that they do not need lifting to overwinter indoors – cardinalis with bright-red foliage and flowers grows to 60cm (2ft) and displays from July to August; *syphilitica*, light blue and only half the height goes on flowering for a month longer.

Lysichitum (Skunk Cabbage) (B): Striking bog plant with large glaucous leaves; likes rich deep mud, takes time to establish and flower. Variety *americanum* has yellow blooms similar in shape to the Arum Lily; *camtschatcense* has pure-white flowers.

Mimulus (Monkey Musk) (B or M): Ever popular and available in a number of varieties, the attractive green foliage a perfect foil to masses of cheerful flowers in yellow, orange, pink and red shades. Give them damp feet and a good sunny position, and they will go on smiling for three or four months from June onwards. All grow between 15–60cm (6–24in) high; *cardinalis* (M) is bright orange scarlet; *bartonianus* (M) has a more rosy-pink glow; *luteus* (B or M) has bright-yellow flowers.

Peltiphyllum peltatum (B & M): Large heads of pink flowers in spring, well before the handsome foliage – a large rounded umbrella shape 1m (3ft) high – appears.

Primulas (M & B): One of the biggest plant families. Not all are suitable for bog gardens, but enough are to provide a selection problem through embarrassment of riches (see Photo 32). They provide almost all colours in the rainbow, flowering from March to July or August. With very few exceptions, do not normally grow above 60cm (2ft) and prefer partial shade.

Denticulata, the drumhead primula, grows to about 30cm (1ft), producing round heads of mainly blue flowers in March. At the other extreme, *florindae* has heads of sulphur-yellow flowers waving 60cm (2ft) above the crowd in June and July. Between these, at a random choice are: *alpicola* comes in white, yellow or purple; *bulleyana*, glorious yellow orange; *capitata*, violet; *halleri*, a lavender-coloured dwarf at only 23cm (9in); *involucrata*, creamy white; and a range of *japonica* in white, crimson or purple. There are many other varieties of various colours and shades.

Rheum (M): A contrast in colour with giant rhubarb-like leaves. All varieties have small flowers of white or pink around May, carried on large impressive flower spike which may be 1·8–2·4m (6–8ft) high with a leaf spread of up to 1·8m (6ft); but not all are as big as this. They take time to establish and are best treated as specimen plants. *Rheum palmatum rubrum* – its early foliage is reddish brown – is the most handsome.

Trollius (Globe Flower) (M): Has dark-green foliage and a mass of large rounded buttercup-like flowers, mostly growing to about 60cm (2ft) in May (see Photo 35). 'Canary Bird' and 'Orange Princess' carry their own colour identity: *pumilus* is a miniature, golden in colour, only 15cm (6in) high and flowering in June and July.

15 The Rockery

CONSTRUCTION

It is one of the fallacies of horticulture that a rockery (or rock garden as the purists insist on calling it) should be in the driest of areas; and it is a fair assumption that many, if not most, of them exist merely because they are a convenient way of hiding old bricks and rubble that have accumulated either during building or over the years. It is a natural line of thought that, with such unpromising material for the base, there is little need or incentive to devote much attention to it.

In practice, however, a rockery is the ideal partner to a pool, certainly as the frame for a waterfall (Fig 63). The mound from which it is formed is easily established from the soil dug out to make the pool and, being adjacent, saves labour in its making. Since on a rockery the amount of soil is limited to pockets between the stones, dwarf plants are best suited for this situation. These enhance the scene forming the perfect contrast or balance; the rockery becomes the natural backcloth to the

pool, and there can be few more harmonious marriages in garden design.

Ideally, waterfall and rockery should be constructed together; it is far more convenient and time-saving in the long run than to make

Photo 36 A natural effect achieved by a watercourse running through a rockery into a pool

Fig 63 A rockery with a waterfall running through is an ideal addition to the pool, the mound from which it is formed is easily established from the soil dug out to make the pool

142

two separate jobs. For a perfect combination they must appear to be part of one unit, so the stones used should be of the same type. Some individual stones will be best suited to the watercourse and others will look better in the rockery; selection and placing is much easier if the whole construction is being worked-on as a complete package.

Before ordering your materials plan your campaign. First, decide how big and exactly where you want the rockery to be. One metre (3ft) will be ample height for most gardens; you will need a lot of soil and rubble if you take it much higher, and you don't need a tower, which would look like a badly disguised spoil heap. A tall rockery would also dry out very easily in a hot summer. Width and depth will depend on the general layout. Keep a sense of proportion. The overall frontage should not be less than three times the height; you are aiming to give the impression of an outcrop of rock.

Next decide the density of rock and, particularly, how much to order. If you were making a stone wall you would need about a ton of stone for every $3 \cdot 2m^2$ (35sq ft) of facing. Reckon on half this density for the rockery and you will be somewhere near right (this is, of course, additional to what you will need for the watercourse). Weight and density of stone does vary, and this can affect your calculations, but normally the difference is marginal. But your sums will not be straightforward for, unlike in a wall, at least a quarter of each stone will be hidden from view securely embedded in the soil, and if you want it to look really natural you will have to make allowance for this.

Some stone, notably Westmorland in England, has a very prominent grain or strata and matching the pieces perfectly is a task that taxes both strength and patience. Frankly, there is some merit in leaving this stone to the professional experts, who have the experience and also large stocks from which they can select each rock individually. It is possible for

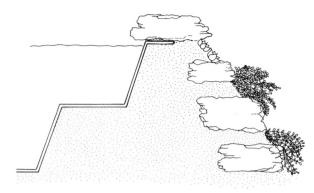

Fig 64 A raised pool can be supported by a retaining rockery with rockery plants between the stones

the amateur to construct an excellent rock garden using this type of stone if particular attention is given to choosing the rocks and keeping the strata parallel; but there are other, less complicated, types that do not pose quite so stern a challenge.

The type of stone you use is important. A good plan is to study your local topography and establish what is the predominant local rock. If you order this you will not only have a 'traditional style outcrop', you will also get it much cheaper than imported stone. I have bitter memories of transport charges more than doubling the cost of the materials I once ordered!

Whatever you buy, be careful how you order. If possible, specify the actual weight of the main pieces you want: it is not amusing to order a ton of stone and find four pieces each of 250kg (5cwt) deposited on your drive. You will need some fairly large ones, of course. Don't try lifting and carrying them and dumping them into the soil at approximately where you want them. You will find it much easier to move the stones if you put planks down first, and a crowbar will be useful for final positioning of each rock. Avoid walking over the mound any more than you can help, as this will compact the surface.

Before starting work, spend a little time studying how experts have gone about the task as part of a water garden. You can learn a lot about structure and design by visiting specialist suppliers and seeing how they have laid out their demonstration rock gardens and ponds, and the temporary displays set up for Chelsea and Southport flower shows will provide a host of ideas. Failing this, there must be a local park or botanical garden with a lake where a large-scale artificial arrangement of stones or rocks has been laid out so well that it looks natural.

Study each piece before you attempt to move it. You are, in effect, building a three-dimensional jigsaw puzzle; while each piece does not have to slot into its neighbour, it must match as near as possible. Study the grain, or strata, and keep each piece horizontal, with the grain foremost; this is what creates the attractive appearance. The work must not be completely symmetrical; this would look hopelessly contrived. Some pieces can be set at a facing angle; this will look natural and provide exposure to the sun and/or shade for various plants at different times during the day. Never set stones going uphill or down; just tilt them slightly so that the front is higher than the back, to retain soil and water. Keep the size of the stones in proportion to the rockery and this in turn in proportion to the pool and the general garden layout. As with the waterfall, start at the bottom and work your way up, cutting into the mound and setting each layer of stone higher and behind the previous one (Fig 65).

The stones themselves will have to be firmly bedded in. Although it is not necessary to cement them into place, as in the pool or watercourse, they must be partly buried and the soil immediately surrounding them well firmed. If you have a watercourse running through the rockery, the falls will act as natural steps between the levels. The rockery layers should follow the same pattern and contour (Fig 66).

One point to watch is soil washing down into the pool. Wherever the rocks hold back

Fig 65 The rockery stone should be laid in tiers

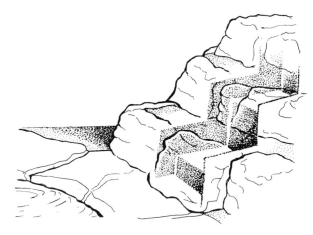

Fig 66 The steps of the waterfall will follow the layers of the rockery

Photo 37 The rockery and waterfall have established and the units blend naturally with the stone

the soil and there is this risk, the stones should be laid close together on a bed of mortar and the gaps between the rocks cemented to retain the soil. Use the cement at the back so as not to destroy the features of the rock face.

You should have saved the topsoil from your excavations to become the planting medium, but it is most unlikely that you will be able to use it without some additions. Rock plants, as distinct from bog plants, need good drainage, which means a fairly coarse open soil, with plenty of grit. Most of the plants prefer neutral or acid soils, so be prepared to add grit and peat or composted bark.

CHOICE OF PLANTS

Although your work in setting the stones will also set the scene, it is the choice of plants that will provide the finishing touch. Planting can, in fact, be the most difficult part, for what you do now will make or break the effect.

Personal choice must play a big part in your selection. It is your garden after all, and it must express your individuality, not conform to a regime. But you will still be restricted by local conditions. For instance, the size of rockery will govern plant growth and therefore, to some extent, the choice of plants you can use.

There are so many plants – many hundreds of varieties – that can be grown in a rockery that discussing them would fill a book. All I can do here is to give a brief outline of various

145

groups, but naming a few varieties that I know have been successful, and so providing a basis for a pleasing finished effect.

Alpines

There is an enormous choice in this section alone, and how useful and attractive they are. They are extremely versatile, thrive in a wide range of conditions, surviving frost and drought, and seem to need very little attention. They fill small pockets of soil, cascade over rocks, hide unsightly features such as pipes, and present an unbelievable combination of delicacy in colour and toughness in growth. The following selection is far from exhaustive but will provide a good basis.

Alyssum: One of the best-loved rockery and edging plants; reputed to be most at home on lime, but will grow almost anywhere provided it gets plenty of sun and has good gritty well-drained soil; *saxatile*, with yellow flowers, is perhaps the best known, spreads rapidly; also try *spinosum*, a dwarf shrubby type with masses of pink or white flowers.

Armeria (Thrift): Grows wild all round the coast; *maritima* (Sea-pink) is probably best variety for rockeries; there are several versions in white or pink, growing from 10–30cm (4–12in).

Aubrieta: Forms a hopelessly overworked double act with Alyssum, but is seen in so many millions of gardens that there cannot be much wrong with such a combination for spring and early summer. Many varieties from pink to deep purple, all growing to about 15cm (6in).

Campanulas: Come in several versions, with saucer-shaped flowers in white or blue, growing from only 5cm (2in) up to 30cm (12in).

Gentians: Flower in late summer as a beautiful blue cloud. Low-growing, but liking a fair amount of moisture. Some experts recommend them also for the bog garden; *sino-ornata* at 15cm (6in) is probably the best, but definitely hates lime; *septemfida* (slightly

taller) is more tolerant.

Helianthemum (Sun Rose): Buttercup-like flowers in all colours except blue. Needs sun, will even thrive in poor gritty soil, and grows well if cut back after first flowering. Most grow about 23cm (9in) high and up to 45cm (18in) spread. 'Red Orient' and 'Raspberry Ripple' are good varieties.

Phlox subulata (Moss Phlox): A good spring-flowering variety in white, pink or mauve, growing to only 10cm (4in) but spreading well.

Sedum (Stonecrop): Creeps and drapes over rock walls, and likes either full sun or some shade. Many varieties, mostly evergreen with small flowers.

Sempervivum (House Leek): Appears in so many varieties it can be classed as a universal dwarf for all purposes. Attractive rosettes of leaves in a wide range of shadings; barely 50cm (2in) high with small flowers that appear in clusters.

Thyme: Very easy to grow, hardy, and evergreen; *coccineus* is only about 7cm (3in) high; *citriodorus*, lavender in colour but lemon in scent, grows to 23cm (9in), spreads to 45cm (18in).

Heathers (Ericas)

These are ideal ground-cover plants for the rockery with attractive foliage and flowers; carefully selected they can give colour throughout the year. All heathers prefer a neutral to acid soil, so have a plentiful supply of peat.

Erica calluna vulgaris: Largest group in the heather family mostly flowering from August to October. 'H. E. Beale' is the best known of the older varieties although there are many new introductions which are considered

Page 147 A simple fountain looks delightful at night when illuminated

146

better. 'My Dream' (white) and 'Anne Marie' (pink), are worth mentioning.

Erica carnea: These varieties will tolerate lime, and flower throughout winter and spring. 'King George' has carmine flowers from November to February; 'Springwood White' is in character from December to April.

Erica cinerea: Summer varieties flowering from June to October in a wide range of colours. 'C. D. Eason', a bright rose, is perhaps the best known; 'Purple Beauty' is also worth noting.

Erica vagans: Late summer/autumn varieties of which 'Mrs D. F. Maxwell' (rose pink) is outstanding.

The many varieties with attractive golden foliage look splendid when planted amongst green varieties. 'Bealey Gold', 'Golden Feather', 'Aurea', 'Golden Drop', are ones for the shopping list.

Dwarf Conifers

A versatile and attractive group of plants ideal for use on the rockery. Over recent years many new varieties have been introduced with colours varying from green, blue and golden to the novel white-tipped varieties. Dwarf conifers grow 5–30cm (2–12in) a year so careful choice is essential, taking into account the size of the rockery and their possible development. Growth habit is also important for they can be columnar, pyramidical or horizontal. The range contains so many plants that I can only give a few of my particular favourites.

Chamaecyparis types include a good selection of dwarfs of mainly globular shape: *minima aurea* is bright yellow with compact growth;

pygmaea argentea is bluish green tipped creamy white and will be only 60cm (2ft) after ten years of growth; *nana gracilis* has dark-green foliage in shell-shaped sprays.

Juniperus types are mainly horizontal growers but some like *chinensis pyramidalis* are, as the name suggests, upright growing. This variety will reach 1·8m (6ft) in ten years. *Juniperus horizontalis* are low-growing carpeting varieties. 'Hughes' is an outstanding form with silver foliage. *Juniperus squamata* types grow slightly taller than the *horizontalis*. 'Holger' bears creamy-yellow foliage through the summer, whilst 'Blue Carpet' creates a sheet of intense silver-blue foliage.

Shrubs

For the larger rockery low-growing shrubs form an interesting contrast alongside heathers and conifers. Again the choice is so extensive I can only mention a few.

Acer (Japanese Maples): Superb associates for poolside and rockeries, creating bright-coloured foliage in a range of shape and habit; *japonicum aureum* is slow growing, bearing golden-yellow leaves; *dissectum* 'Garnet' has spreading habit with finely cut purple/crimson leaves; *palmatum 'Ozakazuki'* has bright-green foliage turning to brilliant scarlet and orange in autumn.

Azalea: Japanese Azaleas and dwarf Rhododendrons form extensive families of evergreen spring-flowering plants and present an overwhelming choice. In the Azalea class, 'Nico' is an excellent variety with masses of cherry-red flowers contrasting well with the white variety 'White Lady'. Of the dwarf Rhododendrons, 'Scarlet Wonder' has a compact mounded habit bearing masses of ruby-red flowers; 'Curlew' has lemon-yellow flowers; 'Dora Amateis' is white.

Berberis: There are several dwarf forms. Try 'Little Favourite' (almost thornless) with purple foliage and orange-yellow flowers.

Cotoneaster: Several dwarf forms; *congestus*

Page 148 (above) Illumination gives an extra dimension to this bell fountain; *(below)* a dramatic effect achieved by different-coloured lights playing on this rockery, waterfall and pool

with creeping habit and bright-red berries throughout autumn is ideal among rocks.

Daphne: These fragrant flowers are a 'must'; *mezereum* is the most famous and you will probably have it in the garden already. For the rockery try *cneorum*, of low-growing habit and bright-pink scented flowers.

Bulbs

Bulbs form a large part of the spring flowering display and need no real introduction. Again, an extensive selection of rockery types exists, including dwarf Daffodils, Tulips, Crocus and Irises for bright splashes of colour from February to May.

Planting Season

All the plants mentioned, except bulbs, are usually container grown and generally available from a garden centre. As they are container grown they can be planted at any time of the year, although in summer they will need watering regularly until they have established.

16 Fish: Varieties and General Care

THE POOL ENVIRONMENT

For all the beauty and colour of plants and the magic of moving water, the factor that really brings a water garden to life is fish. They combine colour, movement and grace in a way that no other aspect of gardening can remotely approach. Without fish, there is something missing from even the most skilfully constructed pool and surround. Their almost ceaseless activity is a source of quiet restful relaxation for any onlooker.

Ornamental cold-water fish are resilient creatures that have minimal requirements – well-oxygenated and unpolluted water, adequate food and freedom to swim. If these basic needs are lacking or if there is a sudden change in environmental conditions, the fish will be under stress, which will make them prone to illness and disease.

Crystal-clear water does not necessarily mean it is suitable for fish. Ensure that the water used to fill the pond has not been stored in metal containers such as a hot-water tank, or delivered through new copper tubing, for dissolved metal ions are toxic to fish. Likewise, metal ornaments (especially lead) should not be present. Take care, too, when using insecticides or weedkillers near the pool, as spray-drift or rainwater running over the treated lawn and into the pond could be disastrous. Soil used in the planting crates should also be free from chemicals. Concrete can be blamed for many troubles. A concrete pool or waterfall improperly treated, rain running over a concrete path into a pool, or cement dust blown from building works, are additional but largely unsuspected hazards – the lime from the concrete dissolving in the water causing a rise in the pH value.

When water contacts untreated concrete, an alkaline solution is formed which can be measured by taking the pH reading – pH testing kits are widely available, inexpensive, and a good investment. On a scale of 0 to 14, a pH of 7 is neutral, above 7 is alkaline and below is acid. The more concrete dissolved, the higher the pH, and this is very harmful, not only to fish but also any animals or birds that may drink from the pond. Therefore it is absolutely essential that all concrete work in and around the pool should be treated with a sealing agent, available from most water-garden centres. Provided that the pH is between 6·5 and 7·5 fish should experience little stress when they are introduced into the pond.

Two weeks before introducing fish, the pool must be planted, special care being taken to include the correct number of oxygenators. This gives the plants time to root, and also allows the pond to become populated with organisms that not only purify the water, but turn a water-filled hole in the ground into a 'pond' with its own tiny environment, and containing its own food system.

Similarly to an area of land being able to maintain a certain number of animals, a pool or lake will support only a given number of fish. This must be taken into account when stocking the pool. Oxygen is the all-important element that limits not only the number of fish but also the life in the pond responsible for breaking down waste matter. As oxygen is absorbed at the surface, the surface area dictates the amount of fish the pond can support.

If stocking a pool for the first time, I would advise that you regard 2·5cm (1in) of fish length per ·09m² (1sq ft) water-surface area as a maximum. After a couple of months more fish can be introduced up to a maximum of 5cm (2in) per same area. There is a reason for this stocking in two stages. Fish, like all living creatures, release into their environment substances that the body no longer needs, either food that cannot be broken down or waste products of body metabolism. Predominantly this is in the form of ammonia, which is passed out through the gill membranes and dissolves in the surrounding water. (In animals, ammonia is discarded from the body in the urine.) Ammonia is an extremely toxic substance, and if this were to accumulate in the pond water, the fish would quite simply poison themselves. Fortunately nature has provided an answer – microscopic organisms called bacteria or, to be more exact, in this case nitrifying bacteria. These bacteria abound in the water itself, on plants, stones and even the pool liner. They depend very largely on the waste matter produced by the fish, which they turn into nitrate, a plant food that is quickly absorbed by plants, notably oxygenators.

There is thus a form of community flourishing together. As the fish grow and produce more waste matter, so the bacteria thrive and multiply. The ecological balance is maintained; the bacteria are present in numbers almost directly in proportion to the waste products produced by the fish. If you suddenly overload this form of ecology by introducing a comparatively large number of fish all at once, you will upset the ecological balance. There is a sudden vast increase of waste matter with which the bacteria cannot cope; they take time to multiply and cannot achieve miracles overnight. The water becomes polluted, the fish lose their appetite (and possibly their colour), and a disease situation could follow.

I have admittedly over-simplified the story to emphasise the dramatic ill-effects that can result from a casual or careless approach to the art of keeping fish in a garden pond, but the message is clear – stock the pond gradually.

Besides this, should there have been an oversight in the construction of the pond resulting in the death of the first introduction of fish, the loss will not be so great, and the problem can be rectified without too much distress. Using 5cm (2in) length of fish per ·09m² (sq ft) surface area as a final stocking guide, allows plenty of capacity for them to grow and multiply.

As fish become semi-dormant in low temperatures, they have very little resistance to stress and subsequent diseases in winter. During this time they should be moved as little as possible so, in northern temperate climates, stocking should only be carried out in the warmer months of April to September.

The growth of most ornamental fish is governed by the size of their environment. An example of this extraordinary situation is that a goldfish in a bowl will reach only a certain length, but move it to a bigger bowl, or give it comparative freedom in a pool, and it can soon double its size.

VARIETIES OF FISH
Goldfish
When the number of fish the pool can support has been calculated, suitable varieties can be chosen. The most common pool fish, and one that automatically springs to mind is the Goldfish, whose ancestry can be traced to China. It most probably first appeared as a coloured mutation of a farmed edible fish which, by careful breeding and selection, resulted in the Goldfish as a species (*Carassius auratus*) being established. In turn, various mutations have been bred and selected, resulting in a vast number of new strains, some of which look nothing like the usual goldfish. Unfortunately, the more exotic the mutation selected, the less hardy the strain developed from it. Consequently only a few goldfish varieties are suitable for outdoor ponds, and some of these only in semi-tropical areas.

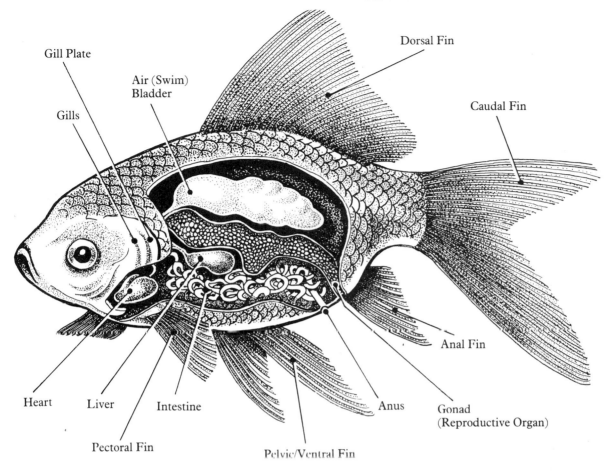

Gill Plate

Air (Swim)
Bladder

Gills

Dorsal Fin

Caudal Fin

Heart

Liver

Intestine

Anus

Gonad
(Reproductive Organ)

Anal Fin

Pectoral Fin

Pelvic/Ventral Fin

Fig 67 Basic anatomy of goldfish

The goldfish is fully scaled except for the head and fins, and although usually gold as the name suggests, it also appears in black, white and yellow colours. The scales are embedded in the skin or dermis, and are interlocked like tiles on a roof. Covering this is the epidermis, which contains numerous secretions capable of killing a wide range of potential parasites. Although the scales are transparent, they are usually backed by a substance that gives the goldfish a metallic look.

In one variety of goldfish, the shubunkin, the scale backing is missing so that the scales become almost invisible, allowing pigment cells lying deeper in the skin to be seen. Although there are only four pigments – black, red, yellow and orange – these can produce a range of colours depending on the cells'

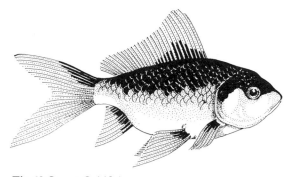

Fig 68 Comet Goldfish

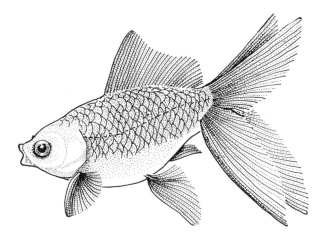

Fig 69 Fantail Goldfish

depth in the skin and the extent to which they overlap each other. For example, the deeper in the skin the black pigment cells are, the more blue they appear.

The common goldfish and shubunkin have short fins: two just below the gills (pectoral fins), a further pair set slightly further back (pelvic fins), a fin just behind the anus (anal fin), and at the very back a tail (caudal) fin. On the back of the fish, starting approximately one-third of the way along, lies the largest (dorsal) fin (Fig 67).

A slight variation occurs in the Comet Goldfish which, although often slimmer, is distinguished from the common variety by having extended pectoral and pelvic fins, and a long flowing caudal fin (Fig 68). Likewise, there is a similar shubunkin variety, the Comet Shubunkin. A recent variation is the Sarasa Comet – a white fish with blood-red markings, which makes it easily visible in a pond and consequently very popular.

The varieties mentioned so far grow to a maximum size of approximately 38cm (15in), but breed when they reach 12 to 15cm (5 to 6in), and are extremely hardy.

Other more exotic goldfish varieties are suitable only for semi-tropical climates or aquaria, and rarely exceed 20cm (8in) when fully grown. These include the Fantail which has a body shaped like an egg and differs from the normal goldfish in that it has a long double caudal fin, which from the back appears as an

Fig 70 Veiltail Goldfish

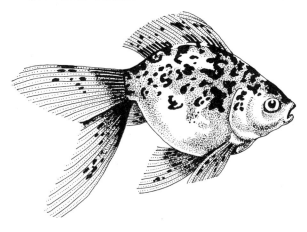

Fig 71 Fantail Shubunkin

Fig 72 Black Moor

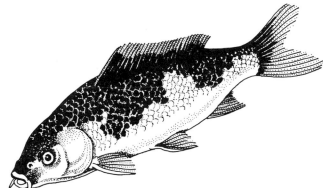

Fig 73 Koi Carp

inverted 'V' (Fig 69). Similar to the Fantail, but with much longer fins – the caudal fin so large it falls in folds – is the Veiltail, an extremely prized but delicate fish (Fig 70).

The Veiltail and Fantail appear not only in shubunkin (calico) form (Fig 71), but also in a black form with bulbous protruding eyes known as a Black Moor (Fig 72). A further variation on the Veiltail is the Oranda which, although the same shape, has a growth or 'hood' on its head. Alternatively, 'hooded' fish may not have a dorsal fin, and so become a 'lionhead' or 'ranchu'. Many more goldfish varieties exist, but often these are too delicate for an outdoor pool even in a tropical climate.

Koi Carp

Koi would seem to be the ideal fish for a conventional garden pond, being extremely colourful and very active. They are a true carp and unfortunately have a tendency, when they are larger, to uproot and eat oxygenating plants. To be on the safe side it is advisable to purchase small Koi for the normal garden pond. Even then, due to their oxygen requirements, they should only be considered for the larger pond with a surface area in excess of 5·6m² (60sq ft). Unlike other ornamental pond fish, Koi are capable of outgrowing a pool, and their size is not so limited by the volume of water.

Koi become sexually mature when they reach a length of approximately 30cm (12in). In perfect conditions they can reach a size in excess of 90cm (36in), although specimens in temperate countries rarely exceed 76cm (30in). When Koi reach 30cm (12in), they are really impracticable in garden ponds and are suitable only for large expanses of water.

There is, however, a special type of pond in which Koi can be kept, often in fairly large numbers emphasising their impressive size and colours. These ponds constructed specifically for Koi are devoid of aquatic plants, and are always built in conjunction with a filter system (see Chapter 7).

When buying Koi carp, you will find the price depends not only on the size of the fish but also on their colours and just as importantly, the definition of those colours – often they can be divided into varieties by their colour and scale group alone (Fig 73). The deeper the colours, and the more exact the pattern, the more valuable the fish. Remember, however, that you are not selecting for the show bench, so the best advice is to buy fish that look attractive to you.

Not all Koi are fully scaled. There is a type that has no scales except a row along the sides and back. These are known as Doitsu, but you may also find them referred to as 'German'. One variety, Shusui – an attractive overall pale

155

blue in colour – comes only in the Doitsu or German form, but other types may be either normal or Doitsu-scaled. Another blue variety, the Asagi, is fully scaled; but here the edges of the scales are paler, producing an unusual net-like effect. There is also a gold-coloured Koi with a pronounced metallic sheen. Known as Ogon it is available in either fully scaled or Doitsu versions.

If you like black in a fish, here, too, the Koi can provide a brilliant example. There are at least three versions known as Utsuri: Ki Utsuri is yellow on black, Shiru Utsuri is white on black and Hi Utsuri is black with red markings. Somewhat confusingly, there are also other varieties where these colourings are reversed. Shiro Bekko is mainly white with black patterns; Aka Bekko is predominantly red with black markings.

This is by no means the end of the main colour combinations. Notably, there is a red and white variety, called Kohaku, which the Japanese regard as the king of Koi. Not surprisingly, for the white fish with its well defined, deep-red markings is a strikingly beautiful specimen. For perfection, the white must be pure, with no specks or flecks.

Another predominantly white fish is the Taisho Sanke. This has smaller areas of red, plus touches of black. It often appears in the Doitsu form.

Other Varieties

Another extremely popular pool fish is the Golden Orfe (Fig 74). These are salmon coloured, with a shape similar to that of a Trout, and are extremely active and easy to see in the pond (see page 130). They can reach a length approaching 50cm (20in) and are best kept in ponds over 5·6m² (60sq ft) surface area, due to their high oxygen requirements. Small Orfe are extremely gregarious and move around the pond in a shoal, although when they reach a size of approximately 12cm (5in) they become more individual. The disappointment with Orfe is that they are extremely difficult to breed.

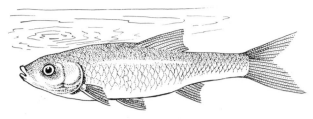

Fig 74 Golden Orfe

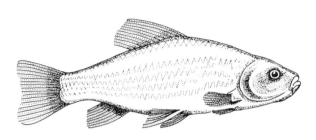

Fig 75 Tench

Almost identical in shape to the Orfe, but usually much darker with red fins, is the Golden Rudd. When small these also form attractive shoals, although they are usually not so easy to see as the Orfe.

Tench are often recommended for pond purposes for two main reasons: one is that they are scavengers, keeping the bottom of the pool clean, and the other that they have therapeutic value for other fish (Fig 75). In fact the Tench is known as the 'doctor fish' – a reputation that is probably vastly overrated. At one time it was thought that damaged fish rubbed against its copious mucus to obtain a cover for their wound until it healed, but there is no evidence to support this theory.

Tench may well scavenge, but they spend most of their time on the bottom of the pool, stirring up the mud. Of the two varieties, green and gold, the gold appears particularly attractive; but the colour makes little real difference, for they are likely to go straight to the bottom of the pool and for all practical purposes will never be seen again.

156

Many anglers often wish to add coarse fish to their pool population. On balance it is better to resist this temptation since various diseases can be introduced and many species such as Perch and Stickleback are aggressive. In addition, their coloration make them difficult to see in the garden pool.

OBTAINING YOUR FISH

Having decided which fish to stock, it is now time to obtain them. Fish keeping as a hobby has grown rapidly in the past few years, with the result that countries with long hot summers have found breeding and growing ornamental fish a profitable business. Israel, Japan, China and the USA export millions of fish each year, despatching them in polythene bags containing minimal amounts of water and inflated with oxygen. These are then packed in cardboard cartons and flown all over the world. In such conditions it is very easy for parasites to multiply and find new hosts, so on arrival at the suppliers they must receive expert treatment in a quarantine area. Only when they have recuperated completely from their journey should they be placed on sale. As pond keepers have neither the space nor expertise to quarantine fish, the choice of supplier is extremely important.

Suppliers normally display fish in tanks that have a continuous flow of water through them. More often than not the water is recirculated through a filter bed and aerated before passing through the tanks again. With such systems, a fairly large number of fish can be kept in a small area.

When choosing fish, ensure that they are active and that all the fins are well spread out, with the dorsal fin erect. Beware of any that are covered in a multitude of white spots the size of a pinhead, or any that appear damaged. Fluffy white patches on the body or the fins usually indicate fungus disease (Fig 76). This is not contagious, so an individual fish will not infect the others in the tank. Remember also that many goldfish have white markings which

Fig 76 Fungus Disease

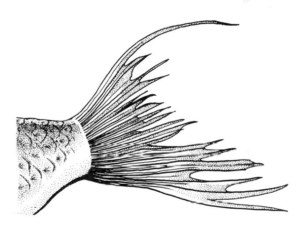

Fig 77 Fin Rot

must not be confused with fungus; but if you have any doubts it is safer not to take a chance. Fin rot is another fairly common problem, causing the edge of the fin to take on a ragged or shredded appearance (Fig 77).

There are other reasons why a fish may be off colour. Treatments are discussed in Chapter 17, but for the moment the advice is to reject any prospective purchases that show any of the symptoms outlined above.

In all probability, your fish will be packed for you in a polythene bag as described, but in far smaller numbers. If the journey home is more than half an hour, you should ask the supplier to inflate the bag with oxygen and, for the journey, the fish should be kept cool and preferably in the dark to calm them and reduce stress. On no account should they be left where the sun can beat down on them.

As fish do not like sudden temperature changes, never release them straight into the pond. Instead, float the bag on the water surface (covered with newspaper to keep out the sun's rays) for about half an hour to allow the temperature in the bag to equate with that of the pool. Then carefully release them. They will probably go straight to the bottom and you won't see them for a couple of days or more. Don't worry; this is a normal reaction. I have heard of Golden Orfe, which normally stay near the surface, staying down for a month or two.

When introducing new fish to an established community, bring in a few at a time – they will be the most stressed and the first to die if there is any trouble. The pH level is especially important in these circumstances. For example, fish can stand fairly large changes of pH provided these occur slowly. An established pond may have had a pH drift over several months to a level new fish could not tolerate, but to which the resident population has adapted.

Above all, do not overstock; half a dozen healthy and active fish are much better than twenty weaklings. Give your fish as much natural shade as possible – water-lily leaves score heavily here and floating plants are also essential. Make sure they have plenty of oxygen, even to the extent of keeping the fountain/waterfall going all night during a summer heatwave to maintain water movement and produce oxygen. The latter is a life saver, not a waste of a unit or two of electricity.

Good preparation of the pool as previously outlined, sensible buying and careful management, will result in many years of splendid enjoyment from your fish.

FEEDING

Fish are cold-blooded creatures and so are unable to maintain a constant body temperature. Instead this is directly controlled by their environment. Consequently they are active in warm weather, but very sluggish in cold, with a corresponding change in their need for food.

During winter, in temperate climates, fish usually find the deepest part of the pool and remain there almost in a state of hibernation. Supplementary food should not be given, unless there is a prolonged warm spell. The temptation to feed them on a single warm day must be resisted. Often, the water warms up enough for the fish to accept food, but the rapid drop in temperature in the evening prevents proper digestion, which leads to food remaining in the gut for a considerable time, with subsequent problems.

During the warmer summer months fish are very active and require feeding; but in extremely hot weather, when water temperatures exceed 27°C (80°F), supplementary feeding in fully stocked ponds should be stopped. This is because the falling oxygen content of the water cannot meet the requirements of the fish as they digest the food.

There is considerable misconception about the feeding habits of ornamental fish, and which supplementary feed is required; a large part of the diet will actually come from within the pond itself. Soon after it is filled, the water becomes populated with many different minute animals, and plants such as algae. Some attach to the pond base, to gravel and to the larger green plants, usually oxygenators. They are a natural food source, and this is the main reason why ornamental fish suck in pebbles or parts of plants and spit them out again; it is simply to obtain the food that is attached.

Fish that have been placed in a new pond often go to the bottom, not only because their surroundings are new to them, but also because that is where most of their natural food exists. So do not be upset, having introduced new fish into a pool, if initially they seem totally uninterested in the food you are offering. Unless the pool is extremely large natural food will, however, become harder to find, and the fish will then require some form of supplementary diet.

Fish should be fed once or twice a day, with sufficient to be consumed in approximately ten minutes. Any uneaten after this time should be netted off, otherwise it will soon sink and decay causing pollution of the water. By feeding the fish in the same place and at the same time each day they will soon become tame. It is also a good opportunity to observe them for any signs of damage or disease.

Feeding fish in Koi ponds requires a slightly different approach. Due to the constant flow of water, and the lack of oxygenating plants, there is very little natural food present in the pond. It does exist, but in this case it is concentrated in the biological filter. Koi, like goldfish, do not have a true stomach, and can digest only small amounts of food at a time. In addition, Koi ponds are designed to maintain a larger number of fish than normal, so that Koi need feeding three or four times a day with a wide variety of food (but in small amounts) to maintain them in a healthy condition. Here more than anywhere the golden rule of fish-keeping applies – feed little, but often.

Many proprietary brands of fish food are available. The main problem is that as soon as the food is processed into a particular form, some of the nutrients are lost due to a number of factors, but mainly to certain compounds becoming oxidised. For this reason, many companies add their own special additives during manufacture to compensate. This is perfectly adequate for garden-pond fish, which can obtain other food from their environment. In Koi ponds, however, where there is no natural supplement, it is safest to feed as wide a range of food as possible, at the same time using a well-manufactured type like the 'floating pellet' as a basic diet. This, as the

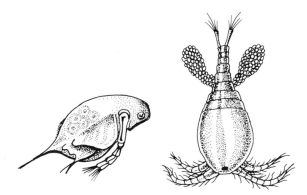

Fig 78 (a) Daphnia   (b) Cyclops

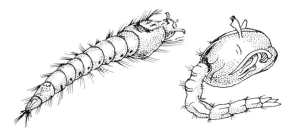

Fig 79 Mosquito larvae and pupa

name suggests, floats in the shape of a pellet; and it can provide most of the dietary requirements of pond fish. A similar food is the floating pond-stick.

The advantage these foods have over most other types is that they float, and this allows any that is uneaten to be easily removed. Fish flake, the type most widely used in aquaria, tends to sink almost immediately; and unless the fish are fed in a shallow area it is difficult to see if it is actually eaten.

The best possible food for fish is crustacea and insect larvae, which they normally obtain from the pond. Many manufacturers, by a special process of freeze drying, have been able to preserve these live foods in a dry form with very little nutrient loss. It is possible to give your fish freeze-dried tubifex, daphnia, shrimp, mosquito larvae, even plankton, but these are much more expensive than the basic diet.

For the more adventurous, these can be caught from natural ponds using a fine net. Small crustaceans such as Daphnia and Cyclops are almost transparent creatures, often tinged red and approximately 3mm (⅛in) long, that abound in stagnant water (Fig 78). Mosquito larvae are found hanging from the water surface, with tufts of hairs along their body (Fig 79). These larvae are about 6mm (¼in) long and wriggle violently if disturbed. The only preparation these foods require is a quick rinse in the net, and the only precaution necessary is not to collect them from polluted water.

Another live food, easily collected from compost heaps, is the earthworm. These can be offered whole, or chopped up. Fish can also be fed on pieces of bread, liver and chopped vegetables; but extra care must be taken with these to ensure that uneaten food is quickly removed before it can pollute the pond.

A problem many garden-pool owners face when going on holiday is what to do about feeding the fish. The simple answer is 'nothing', as fish are able to survive for a long time without additional food. Koi ponds are different, and neighbours may have to be instructed accordingly; but impress upon them that it is better to underfeed than overfeed.

17 Fish: Breeding, Diseases and Predators

SPAWNING AND HATCHING

Most pond fish are not mature and do not breed until they have reached at least 12cm (5in) body length but more usually 15 to 18cm (6 to 7in). With Koi and Orfe the minimum is 25 to 30cm (10 to 12in). In sub-tropical zones, breeding can go on all through the year, but in temperate climates this activity is confined to the summer months.

The first signs that a male is approaching breeding condition is the appearance of raised white lumps, the size of a pinhead and known as tubercles, on the gill plate, and occasionally on the first few rays of the pectoral fins. Females show none of these signs, but a view from above reveals a fattened lower abdomen due to the ovaries filling with eggs, and instead of tapering normally to the tail the body has become fat and lop-sided.

The actual spawning is often triggered by a change in temperature, usually in the period from April to July. It takes the form of a chase, with the female being hotly pursued by two or more males nudging her lower abdomen with their noses, and aiming to force her into the plants growing in the pool. The chase may last for several hours until the female finally releases her eggs – thousands of them – as a long string into the water. The eggs quickly separate, due to both the movement of the water and the fanning action of the fins. They are coated with a sticky substance and adhere to the nearest object, which is usually an oxygenating plant. Those that fail to find a refuge will sink to the bottom, where they will be lost for ever except as food for the other fish and scavengers.

While the eggs are being laid the male simultaneously releases sperm, or milt, which penetrates and fertilises the eggs (or most of them). During spawning the fish often damage themselves and there is nothing the anxious owner can do about it: it is a natural and normal occurrence and usually they recover quite quickly. Exciting, and probably exhausting, as the spawning ritual may be, this brief encounter is the end of the matter so far as the parents are concerned, for they do not rear their progeny. On the contrary, fish eggs and fry are regarded by adults as a live food, so the chances of many offspring surviving are extremely small.

Depending on the water temperature, the eggs will hatch in approximately four days, releasing tiny fry about 6mm (1/4in) long. These attach to oxygenating plants or to the pond sides while they absorb their yolk-sac, which provides them with food for approximately three days. After this the fry become very active and swim to the water surface to fill their swim bladders with air. (If the fry are unable to break the water surface, due perhaps to the presence of a scum, they will soon die.) They then commence feeding on the microscopic food in the pool.

Of the many thousands of eggs laid, and the hundreds hatched from one spawning venture, probably only three or four will survive long enough to reach 2·5cm (1in) in length. Some will have died from weakness; most will have been devoured by insects and other fish, including their own parents. At first, this may appear to defeat the object. However, the threatened population explosion could have

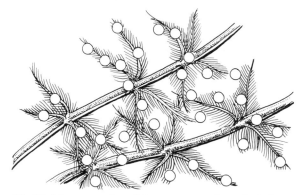

Fig 80 After spawning, fish eggs approximately 1·5mm (¹⁄₁₆in) diameter will be visible on plants

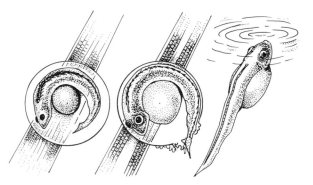

Fig 81 The fry will hatch approximately four days after the eggs are laid

been catastrophic and, when you consider it, three or four newcomers in a normal-sized pool is a very fair rate of increase.

To enlarge your stock more rapidly, and give the eggs a much better start and chance of survival, you can remove them to an appropriate safe receptacle. The eggs are so tiny – only about 1·5mm (¹⁄₁₆in) in diameter – that you must avoid the burning desire to collect them by the hundred (Fig 80).

REARING FRY

For those who wish to rear a few fry out of the confines of the garden pond there are a number of different methods. The easiest of these is, in its simplest form, a miniature pond without any fish or predators present.

Before the fish have spawned, obtain or construct a container about 1m (3ft) square and ·3m (1ft) deep. Fill it nearly to the top with tap water, cover with a fine mesh (net curtain is ideal) and place it in direct sunlight. When the fish have spawned, transfer some of the oxygenating plants with eggs attached into the container. After the eggs have hatched and the fry have absorbed their yolk-sac, they will feed on the plankton and minute crustacea that will have formed in the water (Fig 81).

Do not try to raise too many fry. Approximately a hundred eggs should be transferred

and, when the fry reach 13mm (½in) in length, they should be culled to leave twenty fish. The container should be large enough to support these until they reach 2·5cm (1in) in length, when they can be transferred to the pool, provided that this does not lead to overstocking.

The owner who wants to raise larger quantities of fry needs a more sophisticated approach. The first consideration is to stop the water from becoming polluted and this can only be achieved by having a filtered aquarium system into which the oxygenators, with eggs attached, can be transferred. A special air-operated sponge or under-gravel filter is best for this rearing tank: avoid power pumps as they would be likely to suck up the fry (Fig 82).

The second consideration is the feeding of the fry. As soon as the fish have spawned a special culture will have to be set up ready for the first feed. Fill a saucepan with straw chopped into 5cm (2in) lengths, top up with water and boil for half an hour. When cool, strain the water into a container, and add a few drops of pond water. This should then be stored in a shed or garage in diffused light and there, after three or four days, it will begin to smell, corresponding with the appearance of dust-like particles indicating the presence of Infusoria.

162

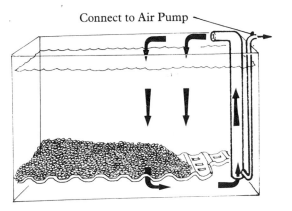

Connect to Air Pump

Fig 82 A small filtered aquarium; water passes through the gravel and is forced up the tube by injecting air

These can be fed to the fry using a drip feed which can easily be constructed using a piece of air-line as a siphon, and an air-line clamp to regulate the flow.

Feeding with Infusoria should start three days after the fish hatch and continue for four or five days, after which time the fry can be fed on Brine Shrimp. These are bought from specialist suppliers as dehydrated cysts – looking like a dry powder – and are reactivated by simple aeration in a salt-water solution made by dissolving 25g of salt per litre of water (1oz to a quart). If you need only a few, pour the water into a tray or dish and sprinkle a few eggs on the surface. Maintain a temperature of 23°C (74°F) and the shrimps will hatch within one or two days. The eggs themselves are dark brown, but when hatched the young shrimps are pale pink in colour and only ·5mm (¹⁄₅₀in) long. They must be thoroughly washed (using a very fine sieve or a nylon stocking) to remove the salt water before being given to the fry.

If you need a larger supply of Brine Shrimp, these can be hatched using an air-pump and a plastic squash-bottle. Cut the bottom off the bottle, stand it on a support with the cone at the bottom. Fill it three-quarters full with the salt solution, aerate from the bottom of the cone and pour in 2 teaspoonfuls of eggs; the movement of air will keep the eggs in suspension. This is essential, for without aeration the eggs would fall to the bottom and form a layer that the oxygen could not penetrate; the eggs would fail to hatch and then decay.

This is one of the best fry foods available and should be fed until the fry are about 20mm (¾in) long, when they can be reared on a mixture of Brine Shrimp and commercially available fry food, available from pet shops. Feed this sparingly but often, 5 or 6 times per day. A good, well-varied diet is necessary; if the fry do not get the proper nutrients in their early stage deformities could result.

Do not be alarmed at what appears to be a colour tragedy. Fry of goldfish varieties are nearly always black, but usually colour up at a later date. This may depend on a number of environmental factors, including temperature and diet.

DISEASES
Cause and Prevention
If their basic needs are provided for, and a little common sense applied when necessary, fish will remain free from most diseases, very few of which are so virulent that they occur spontaneously.

Normally, as with animals and man, most disease-causing agents live harmlessly side by side with the fish and disease symptoms arise only when the fish are under stress of some kind, resulting in a weakening of their immunity system. For example, fish can become ill or diseased during or immediately after the spawning season, simply because they are exhausted and have not recovered sufficiently before a parasitic infection has taken a strong hold.

Examination of the skin of perfectly healthy fish often reveals one or two parasites browsing on dead outer-skin cells. They vary in size from incredibly small microscopic bacteria to larger creatures visible to the naked eye.

163

Potential skin parasites are kept in check by a protective mucous coating that contains various chemicals capable of killing parasites. When the immunity system is suppressed, which is usually due to a change in the environment, once-harmless parasites multiply rapidly and start destroying live skin cells, so the fish become diseased. If the cause can be traced back to a fault in its environment, not only will the disease have to be cured but also the cause rectified.

As previously mentioned, untreated concrete can be a problem due to the lime leaching into the water. Depending on the amount of dissolved lime it can cause irritation in the fish, stripping of the protective mucous coating, or even severe 'burns' leading to death. Other major problems can result from what must be described as bad husbandry. Feeding old or mouldy food would be detrimental; over-feeding can result in food going to the bottom, decomposing and setting up a condition beyond the capacity of the bacteria that normally process pool waste.

Over-stocking the pool is a similar fault. If you have too many fish, or they are larger than your pool was designed to support, they will produce more waste than the bacteria can break down, so the fish will poison themselves. A similar form of pollution results from the build-up of dead and decaying plants, with predictable results. A pool is not a receptacle for waste; if normal garden maintenance is neglected the price will have to be paid.

Garden chemicals are another potential source of danger. Just about every form of manufactured fertiliser, pesticide or insecticide – other than the special formulations for aquatic use – is toxic to fish. Take every possible precaution to prevent sprays reaching the water. Chemicals in liquid or powder form can be carried by the wind, so apply when either there is no wind or when it is blowing away from the pool. Soil-applied chemicals can be leached into the pool if a slope permits, so the wise owner will have sited his pool, as advised,

well clear of any such potential troubles.

Fish placed directly in fresh tap-water will immediately become stressed, due to the chlorine levels in the supply. Ponds that have been left for two weeks will not have this problem, but those that are hurriedly constructed, with fish, water and plants being introduced immediately, are inviting trouble.

In an established pond, especially during hot summer nights, there can be a lack of oxygen. Warm water cannot dissolve as much oxygen as cold and, in addition, plants and algae which produce oxygen during the day absorb it at night. The oxygen content may also fall during thunderstorms because of the low atmospheric pressure, and fish may be seen gasping at the water surface. These conditions can even result in the death of active fish such as Orfe. Fountain or waterfall should be running to ease the situation.

Fish in direct sun can also become sunburnt, so ensure that there is adequate surface cover. Faulty electrical equipment may cause them to swim in a peculiar fashion, or even stun them.

In winter it is essential to keep at least part of the pool free from ice to allow exchange of gases with the atmosphere. Never break ice on a pool as the resulting shockwaves can kill the fish; it must always be melted. An even better method is to use a small pool heater specially designed for this purpose.

Treatments

If fish display an unusual form of activity, such as rubbing against some object in the pool, suspect parasites and act before the infection leads to something more serious.

To examine a fish closely, first net it and remove it to a shallow container filled with pond water. Do not chase it around the pool until it is exhausted; it will be caught more easily by slow and careful movement with the net, especially if tempted to one area with some food. If fish have to be handled, the hands must be wet. Dry hands simply strip them of their mucous coat, leaving them susceptible to infection.

Fungus is one of the commonest disease problems. It appears as a cottonwool-like growth, usually white or grey, but sometimes green due to algae penetration (see Fig 76). It may start anywhere on the body or fins and is rather like a plant in that the fluff (hyphae) is the outside growth sustained by a root system (mycelium) that penetrates the skin. If spotted early it is quite easy to cure – there are plenty of proprietary products, mostly based on malachite green or phenoxethol – but a severe attack is often fatal because the fungus roots will have penetrated too far into the skin. Fungus spores are present in all waters but thrive best where there is little or no current. Disinfecting is no protection, for they are air-borne and may drop anywhere. Dead or decaying matter is a perfect host for fungus moulds.

Another common disease called white spot is caused by *Ichthyopthirius multifiliis* – a small parasite about the size of a pinhead which develops and spreads anywhere on the body of the fish giving the appearance of having been sprinkled with salt. Here too, there are plenty of commercial products to clear the infection.

Fish Lice (*Argulus* sp.) can be a recurring problem. They appear as a jelly-like disc about 6mm (¼in) in diameter, usually with a green centre, normally only on the body but in severe cases also on the tail and other fins (Fig 83). A complication is that the lice lay eggs, and though several proprietary cures will take care of the adults in the pond, the eggs remain unaffected. A course of treatment is therefore necessary, with a series of applications as the eggs hatch.

The Anchor Worm (*Lernaea* sp.) is another skin parasite but this actually penetrates the dermis of the fish resulting in a slightly raised lump. As the parasite matures it produces a white tail about 13mm (½in) long which can be seen on close examination (Fig 84). This one requires very careful handling. Net the

Fig 83 Fish Lice (*Argulus*)

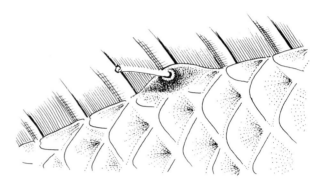

Fig 84 Anchor Worm (*Lernaea*)

fish and carefully remove the worm with tweezers; as it is pulled out it will reveal an anchor-shaped head. Paint the affected area with a disinfectant such as white iodine or 2 per cent mercurochrome, and treat the water with one of the specialist products available.

Another worm-like creature about 2·5cm (1in) long attaches itself to fish. This is the Fish Leech; fairly rare, but encountered occasionally and distinguished by the dark bands around the body. Other leeches do occur, but these feed on insects, snails and plants. There is a selection of commercial cures.

Other parasites, the microscopic ones, present a slightly different problem because their presence is not immediately obvious and they can cause a lot of damage before being recognised. The eccentric behaviour of a fish 'rubbing' against the pool sides may be an indication of their presence. Remove the affected fish, examine it closely, and if there are no obvious signs of other parasitic infection treat in a strong salt bath, 10g per litre (1oz to 6pt). Use ordinary salt, not the iodised type. This bath treatment should last for half an hour, but watch closely and if the fish shows signs of distress or starts to lose its balance return it to fresh water immediately. Pond fish do not like salt water, so don't overdo it: the object is to dehydrate the parasites before the fish is badly affected.

There is a further form of parasite, in the form of microscopical single-celled creatures – bacteria. Often when the skin becomes damaged, bacteria living in the pond become opportunist parasites. The infected area may form a swelling which ruptures, producing a hole in the side of the fish. Dab the area with a 2 per cent mercurochrome solution, or with a commercial remedy containing an antibactericide. In severe cases it may be necessary to ask a veterinary surgeon to administer antibiotics.

Another unpleasant disease is mouth fungus, in which the bacteria eats away at the mouth of the fish. Despite its name this is not fungal infection, but a serious bacterial disease that can spread rapidly. Isolate infected fish immediately and treat as previously described.

You may find an occasional fish with ragged red fins. This is fin rot, another form of bacterial attack, which usually affects only long-finned varieties. This time the remedy is simple – catch the fish and treat with an antibactericide. If the infection is severe trim off the ragged edge of the fin and paint or dab with a 2 per cent mercurochrome solution. When the infection has been cured the fin will regrow.

You may find a fish rolling about, bloated, the scales extended to look like a pine cone, and with bulging eyes. Two possibilities exist. If a single fish is affected, it has probably lost its ability to regulate the water content of the body due to an internal disorder. Although there is no known cure the condition may cure itself. It is not contagious. However, if others show the same symptoms you must suspect infectious abdominal dropsy, which is extremely rare in ornamental fish but is contagious (Fig 85). In the unlikely event of an outbreak of this disease expert advice should be sought.

Fig 85 Dropsy Disease

This covers all the diseases the pondkeeper is likely to encounter. There are other disease-causing agents, but in ornamental pond fish these are so rare that they do not warrant a mention.

Fish, on the other hand, may die due to other factors over which the owner has no control. They have internal organs like other large animals and the failure of any of these to function correctly will bring about eventual death (see Fig 67). Fish that over-eat the wrong food are liable to the same problems of fatty liver and weak heart as a fat person would be.

Similarly, they may develop cancerous tumours in organs with resulting loss of function of the affected part. Some fish are liable to certain disorders due to their shape; for example Fantail varieties occasionally develop swim-bladder trouble which results in their swimming upside down.

Consequently some fish may become debilitated or die in perfect environments, with no outward signs of disease.

ENEMIES OUTSIDE AND INSIDE POOL

Fish may suddenly disappear without trace from a pond, with a simultaneous unnatural shyness in the residual population. This, or unexplained wounds on the body of a fish, can almost certainly be attributed to the presence of predators. Though the scouting Gull is ever ready for a quick snack, by far the greatest menace is the Heron. Even in urban areas, where it is not normally seen during the day, it will frequently arrive at dusk or daybreak looking for a tasty meal. An obvious indication that one has visited a pond is a small area of white wax-like deposit floating on the surface.

It is extremely difficult to dissuade Herons from taking fish. Shooting is impracticable as well as being illegal in most countries, and I know of only one deterrent. A Heron will not land directly into a normal garden pool but will land nearby and wade in; to protect your fish, you can turn this habit to your advantage. Drive in a series of stakes all round the pool and about 30cm (1ft) or so away from it and attach two strands of wire, one 15cm (6in) above the ground, the other about 45cm (18in). It may not look pretty, but it is effective. Obviously in pools that have no shallow areas, a Heron is unlikely to be able to take any fish.

The Kingfisher is another beautiful bird that takes fish as a natural part of its diet. One consolation is that only small fish are at risk. Short of stretching a net all over the water, which has nothing to commend it, there is no known prevention.

Cats automatically come to mind as predators, but with some individual exceptions they are not a major menace. They are not fond of water, and healthy fish are usually too quick even for them. Any victim is likely to be a fish that is sluggish, probably because of an infection or other illness. In rural areas Otters or Snakes may be a problem, but such attacks are very rare and will not affect many pool owners.

Fig 86 Great Diving Beetle: (top) female; (left) larvae; (right) male

Fig 87 Dragonfly

167

Enemies within the pool are a different matter, for there are a number of insects that live in or on the pool and regard fish as their natural prey. The Great Diving Beetle is a real menace, for not only will it eat fry, it is also capable of nipping adult fish, with consequent risk of bacterial infection. Diving-beetle larvae are just as bad, for they 'hang' from the surface of the water with their two large pincers probing for victims (Fig 86). Nymphs of the dragonfly, which are furnished with a powerful hinge-shaped lower jaw, have similar habits (Figs 87, 88). Several other water insects are also capable of attacking fish. One of the most persistent of these is the Water Boatman (Fig 89). The only possible remedy for these insect predators is to net them out of the pond.

Frogs are not predators but the males can be a menace in their mating season. At this time they will cling to virtually anything that moves and occasionally a fish may be the subject of this attention. When this happens the fish is very easy to catch and the Frog can be removed.

Do not be deterred, or perturbed, by this collection of troubles that could arise. I have covered almost everything that might happen but, more than likely, none of it ever will!

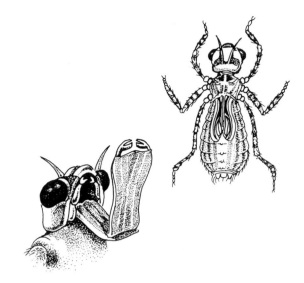

Fig 88 (right) Dragonfly larvae; (left) close-up of larvae head

Fig 89 Water Boatman

18 Lighting the Pool and Garden

THE SIMPLE RULES

Although not strictly horticultural, installing a lighting system can prove one of your most exciting and pleasurable gardening adventures. In effect, it will give you two gardens in one. On warm summer and autumn evenings, it will enable out-of-doors recreation and relaxation to continue long after dusk, and even in cool or wet weather you can still enjoy the view from indoors. What better way of extending and enjoying the use of your garden?

By day, in the full glare of the sun, your eye takes in the complete canvas, with every colour in the garden fighting for recognition. At night, a few lights strategically placed and directed will highlight and dramatise – even romanticise – your garden in the most incredible fashion, and with little effort you can change the setting to emphasise something different every night. Thus you can turn your garden into a form of open-air theatre. Trees, sculptures, shrubs and plants become individual star performers, with part of the stage to themselves. Some will appear to take on different shapes and colours as the lights, sometimes helped by a slight evening breeze, pick out salient features. Fountains and waterfalls become dancing shimmering curtains of colour – colour that can be made to change every few seconds.

The garden is a study in still-life, quiet and placid. But under lights from dusk onwards it is vibrant and full of excitement; there can even be an air of mystery as you come across a plant or other object standing out against the dark background. For, with lighting, you can bring into prominence a subject that may not be particularly noticeable by day. Modern and comparatively inexpensive equipment makes it possible to have a number of lighting circuits, each illuminating half a dozen individual features; and you operate any or all of them by the flick of a switch without even going into the garden. You can watch from inside the house or you can tour the garden, always looking for new ways to dramatise its features. Lighting is, of course, particularly effective if you are staging a barbecue; and although its benefits are chiefly appreciated in summer, you can get astonishing effects in winter, especially after a fall of snow.

Most houses have outside lights for purely practical reasons – lighting doorways, paths and drives is an example. Ornamental lighting in the garden is merely an extension of this principle. The possibilities are unending but, as in most aspects of gardening, there are a few simple rules.

The first is, don't try to flood the garden with light. Full glaring floodlights only ape the sun and don't perform so well. They illuminate, but provide no character or contrast; everything is flattened. Instead, pick out a few items you wish to make prominent, much as you would if composing a photograph or a painting. In general, place your lights on the ground, directed upwards into the tree or whatever you wish to highlight – you can get marvellous dappled effects through the foliage. Careful siting will also help to illuminate pathways, steps or any other potential hazard.

Don't confine your ambitions to normal

Photo 38 Ornamental lamps suitable for outdoors

house-type white light. Experiment with the various colours available and watch the different lighting effects, but choose the softer pastel shades. Pink is a warming colour; so, too, is red. Amber gives highlights, but is less brash and harsh than the normal clear bulb. Green has a softening restful effect. Blue can be effective in some cases, but mainly it is cold and is best used for special purposes such as illuminating moving water.

You will have to experiment with the placing of the lamps – so much depends on the individual item, or items, you are seeking to illuminate. Sometimes you will get a better result by placing your light directly in front of the object; at others you will get a more dramatic picture by lighting from one or even two sides. Backlighting is not very successful as a rule: you cannot 'bounce' light or colour effec-tively by reflection as you can when taking a photograph.

The water garden offers great scope for lighting, either from below water level or at the waterside. Rockeries and waterfalls, because they are raised, can add a new dimension to the night-time scene. Water splashing over the falls can be easily highlighted from the side; even better, if the construction permits, is to site a light directly below or behind an actual waterfall. When lighting a fountain, always light from below, not above. If you can place your lamps directly under the fountain, so much the better; you will get a fantastic effect, for the colour stays within the confines of the water, making it stand out dramatically against the blackness of the night (see page 147). The illumination is carried in the water to the peak of the spray, and the droplets falling back to the pool glisten like sparks. In this situation a pool scores some of

170

its most spectacular points. A single lamp under water can throw a beam an astonishing distance, especially if the water is clear.

Also below the water, you can have lamps for general illumination of the pool. Although this will not be as spectacular as lighting a fountain, it will give an interesting view of the fish and underwater world not always noticed or seen in daytime. Fountain ornament and pool-side figures can be illuminated either from the side or actually in the pool.

There are two ways of installing lighting for your pool, and I strongly recommend incorporating a system for the entire garden while you are about it. One operates off the mains; the other requires a low-voltage transformer which reduces the normal mains down to 12V and makes whatever you do completely safe and harmless. The two systems can, of course, be operated side by side, but independently.

I cannot stress too strongly the need to use only purpose-made lighting systems for outdoor use, especially when installing lights under water.

MAINS VOLTAGE

There are many types of lamp especially made for outdoor use. Some are purely practical, comprising a weatherproof lampholder housing a special sealed lamp and reflector bulb, either clear or coloured (see Photo 40). Others are more ornamental; for example, they can be in the shape of a mushroom, a bollard, or with a clear polycarbonate globe (see Photo 38). As with pumps, all permanent installations must comply with the local Electricity Board and Institute of Electrical Engineers (IEE) regulations in Britain or Institute of Electrical and Electronics Engineers (IEEE) in the United States or the strict regulations of the various state electricity boards in Australia (see Chapter 8). For your own convenience, make sure the wiring leads back to the house, so that you can switch on and off without having to go out into the garden.

Lights run directly off the mains normally

Photo 39 A fountain illuminated from below the jet makes a spectacular display

have much more power than those on a low-voltage circuit. Floodlamps generally have 100W or 150W lamps, but can go up to 500W or more. The ornamental types usually have standard household 60W bulbs. Floodlamp types are normally available with either a base-plate for mounting onto walls, gateposts and copings, or with a spike which simply pushes into the ground. A swivel adjuster is usually incorporated for setting the lamp at the correct angle.

Ornamental types are available in a number of attractive designs which are ideal for integrating into the rockery or herbaceous border. Bollard and lamp-post style lamps are ideal for lining paths as well as borders. For creating a festive air for barbecues, parties and at Christmas there is little to beat the old-style 'fairy lamp' festoon. Nowadays these are usually available in sets of ten 25W bulbs of different colours with a length of cable. Three or four sets can be linked together. A development of this idea has been to house the bulbs in 'lanterns' – also available in sets of ten – and very effective they look.

All these can be laid out within sight of your pool and surround; but although you can train lights onto the pool-side plants, I stress the dangers of their getting too close to water splashing from the fountain or waterfall. If you want the best-on-the-spot lighting for the water, you must have special underwater floodlamps of 100W or 150W, sealed into a special corrosion-resistant unit. These must be kept below the water surface, as it is essential that they run cool. The normal arrangement is for a clear bulb; if you want red, blue, amber or green colour, you buy the appropriate lens. Usually these lenses are perspex and cannot be used above water as the heat will distort them.

I mentioned before about siting a lamp directly below the fountain so that marvellous effects can be obtained. One very popular unit comprises a pump plus a 150W spotlight sealed for underwater use, a jet and a four-colour segmented disc which revolves under the movement of the water to produce a series of automatic colour changes at easily adjustable intervals. Every drop of water is lit from the centre. It provides an enthralling Roman-candle type of spectacle. The most sophisticated equipment of this nature that I have seen enables the owner to have fountains dancing to music, reaching different heights and changing colour by an ingenious device which operates lights and up to sixteen fountain patterns linked to the rhythm of the music. You can buy a lighting set consisting of three lamps mounted on a special base, and you can imagine the effect with three colours playing on a fountain set in their centre.

If you are illuminating a fountain, place the underwater lights as close as possible to the surface, bearing in mind the necessity to keep them cool. If set some inches down and the water is murky, the best effect will be lost; to get the best results the water must be clear. However, do not place the lamp where it is only partially submerged – the part that is above water will get hot while the part that is under water will stay cool, and this can cause stress fractures.

LOW VOLTAGE

This is the big safety factor in garden electrics. A simple (sealed-unit) transformer plugged into the normal mains socket reduces the normal mains voltage to a harmless 12V, which is so safe that you can literally stick metal pins into the live wire without getting hurt. The transformer will get hot when in use so must be kept in a well-ventilated, but dry, place. The garage is a suitable spot to house it: the switch can, of course, be at a convenient point in the house.

Although the lights are naturally more subdued than the powerful floods on the mains circuit, they are fully effective for water features. You are throwing a beam at most 1·5m (5ft) high to show up a fountain or a bush, not aiming for the top of a clock tower. Most low-voltage systems have lamps of 18W or 21W, and a complete circuit of six lamps will run for about ten hours on one unit of electricity. Recently, lighting systems using halogen bulbs have been introduced, and these are claimed to have greater illumination.

There are several types of low-voltage lamp on the market. Most are supplied with about 15m (50ft) of cable, but you are not confined to this length; I have heard of systems using up to 152m (500ft) without any noticeable voltage drop (heavy-duty cable helps here). The major restriction is in the number of lamps you can use off given transformers. Some sets will give you only two lights, others will go up to six – the maximum you can get on the normal transformer though you can buy an industrial transformer, which will operate more.

As with mains lamps, special types – consisting of a sealed lamp in a waterproof housing – are available for underwater lighting. One of these is made so that the lamp will float on the water if required, but can be weighted and sunk to the bottom of the pool. From here it will illuminate the water and plants, or ornaments around the pool, very effectively. It comes with easily changeable coloured lenses.

Two versions are normally available for use in the garden. One has a spike for simply pushing into the ground or a bracket for fastening to a wall; the other is of mushroom type. Both can be supplied with or without transformer and cable.

Photo 40 A floodlamp suitable for use outdoors

The low-voltage cable is heavy duty, but is amazingly easy to use, and does not have to be buried or protected. All you have to do is clamp your lamps into it wherever you wish (two pins pierce the cable). If you wish to move them – perhaps if a rose bush is past its best and you want to illuminate something else – you merely pull out the lamp and clamp it in again where required. The pin-marks that are left in the cable will reseal and give no cause for alarm. Should the cable be damaged, it can be repaired with ordinary insulating tape; and as these systems are so simple and safe you can do all the wiring yourself without paying for professional work.

Acknowledgements

This book germinated during a visit to Nantwich, Cheshire, England, to gain information for a magazine article about Stapeley Water Gardens, the largest water garden centre in Europe, which attracts a million or so visitors a year to its 45 acre site and sells just about every item needed in and for any water garden.

The owners, the brothers Ray and Nigel Davies, had been planning a series of booklets on the different facets of water gardening. They wanted to offer their customers more comprehensive yet more concise information than was currently available, and knowing I had written or edited a number of books on gardening and other subjects asked if I would like to produce the necessary text. Before I left, the overall plan had been agreed.

One of their customers, David St John Thomas, head of the David & Charles publishing group, heard of the project and suggested expanding it into one full-size definitive volume for the thousands of temperate-zone water gardeners world wide. So here it is. An author seldom publicly acknowledges his publisher; I gladly do so, because I know mine has a personal interest in the subject!

While it would be foolish to claim that this book is the last word, I can claim that no book on a specialised garden subject can ever have been produced more enthusiastically or by such a dedicated team. For this has been a team effort, every member a specialist in his or her way. Though I succumbed many years ago to the magic of water and its light and movement and colour and life, for enabling this book to stake its claim for a place in garden literature I owe a tremendous debt to a number of people.

First among them must be Ray and Nigel Davies, who inspired and instigated it and whose own professional experience and knowledge has taught me, guided me, and corrected me where necessary and who have spent many hours on it. Then there is Paul Dykins, whose knowledge of pond fish has been placed freely at my disposal. George Telford, the artist, has brought not only outstanding expertise in remarkably clear technical drawings, but also a proven love of the subject: several photographs are of his own garden.

Behind these four stalwarts lies a group of Stapeley experts who have read and reread the manuscript, checking against errors, suggesting improvements, and generally ensuring that the finished work conveys sound information but also entertains, making a volume that can be picked up at any point but proves hard to put down because the reader, like those who produced it, has become absorbed in the subject.

To all who have so willingly given their time and knowledge I offer my grateful thanks. Without them, this would never have happened.

1985   Stanley Russell

Further Reading

The Complete Guide to Water Plants, Helmut Muhlberg (E.P., 1982)

Cure and Recognize: Aquarium Fish Diseases, Dr Gottfried Schubert (T.F.H. Publications, 1974)

The Goldfish, Hervey & Hems (Faber, 1981)

Goldfish Guide, Dr Yoshiichi Matsui (T.F.H. Publications, 1982)

Koi for Home and Garden, Glen Takeshita (T.F.H. Publications)

Koi of the World, Dr Herbert Axelrod (T.F.H. Publications, 1973)

Nishikigoi Fancy Koi, Takehiko Tamaki (Tamaki Yogyoen, 1974)

Water Lilies, Philip Swindells (Timber Press, 1983)

MAGAZINES

Aquarist & Pondkeeper (monthly)
Practical Fishkeeping (monthly)
Practical Gardening (monthly)
Amateur Gardening (weekly)
Garden News (weekly)
Popular Gardening (weekly)

Useful Addresses

Cement and Concrete Association: 52 Grosvenor Gardens, London SW 1

British Koi Keeper Society: 35 Coppleridge Drive, Crumpsall, Manchester

There are many aquarist societies – one in nearly every large town. Consult local telephone directories.

Further information on any aspects of water gardening:

Stapeley Water Gardens Ltd,
Nantwich,
Cheshire
CW5 7LH

Index

Acknowledgments

Putting together this book would have
been extremely difficult without the help
of Alan Christie, my head chef at Arbutus,
and William Smith, my business partner.

My thanks also go to Colin Kelly at
Wild Honey and all the team there and
at Arbutus, for their dedication and
hard work.

I am also indebted to Alison Cathie,
Jane O'Shea and everyone at Quadrille
for sharing the passion and enthusiasm for
the modern bistro movement.

Last but far from least, I am beholden to
my infinitely patient and painstaking editor,
Lewis Esson, as well as to the book's visionary
designer Lawrence Morton and Simon
Wheeler the gifted photographer, for their
considerable contributions.

First published in 2008 by Quadrille
Publishing Limited, Alhambra House, 27-31
Charing Cross Road, London WC2H OLS

This paperback edition published in 2010

Editorial Director: Jane O 'Shea
Creative Director: Helen Lewis
Editor and Project Manager: Lewis Esson
Art Director: Lawrence Morton
Photography: Simon Wheeler
Production: Marina Asenjo

Text © Anthony Demetre 2008
Photographs © Simon Wheeler 2008
Edited text, design & layout © Quadrille Publishing Ltd 2008

The rights of Anthony Demetre to be identified as the Author of this Work have been asserted
by him in accordance with the Copyright, Design and Patents Act 1988.

Cataloguing in Publication Data: a catalogue record for this book is available from the British Library

ISBN 978 184400 838 4

Printed and bound in China